Inside the Foreign
Exchange Universe

Inside the Foreign Exchange Universe

(An Essential Guide to Forex)

Tholoor M. Thomas, CFA

authorHOUSE®

AuthorHouse™ UK Ltd.
1663 Liberty Drive
Bloomington, IN 47403 USA
www.authorhouse.co.uk
Phone: 0800.197.4150

Published by AuthorHouse   12/20/2013

ISBN: 978-1-4918-8748-6 (sc)
ISBN: 978-1-4918-8753-0 (hc)
ISBN: 978-1-4918-8754-7 (e)

Contents

Preface

Your selection of this book for an enchanting read is greatly appreciated.

The subject of foreign exchange has attracted considerable attention in recent years. Foreign exchange refers to the act of converting one currency into another. Foreign exchange has become part of daily life: directly or indirectly, we are exposed to some sort of foreign exchange, including the impact of volatile exchange rates. Whether you buy a car, a suit, or some dollars for your travel, a foreign exchange transaction is involved. In short, we are susceptible to the daily fluctuations in foreign exchange rates whether we like it or not. The foreign exchange market, which was once accessible only to large banks and financial institutions, is now available to ordinary people.

The foreign exchange market has become the largest financial market among all asset classes. It carries a transaction volume of almost five trillion US dollars per day. The year 1971 will be remembered as the birth of the modern foreign exchange market. During that year, the Bretton Woods Agreement governing the fixed exchange rate system was abolished, and several countries decided to adopt the floating exchange rate system. The market has taken off since then and grown tremendously.

The major players in the foreign exchange market include large banks, financial institutions, commercial banks, sovereign wealth funds, asset managers, hedge funds, and large corporations. The main objectives when undertaking foreign exchange transactions include investment, hedging, and speculation. The foreign exchange market is relatively less regulated. Currency speculation can bring down governments and cause economic chaos, but central banks tend to wield their power and halt excessive currency fluctuations in order to bring stability to the exchange rates.

An understanding of foreign exchange basics and the way the market operates is a precondition for anyone interested in pursuing a career in foreign exchange or participating in any foreign exchange activity. The subject of foreign exchange is much more complex than it appears to be at first glance.

This book is unique in the sense that it encompasses various essential aspects of foreign exchange under one roof, which I perceive as a shortcoming of other books on the subject. I started my career in 1971 in the foreign exchange department of India's largest bank, which was at the forefront of the forex market in India. Incidentally, the start of my career coincided with the onset of the floating exchange rate regime. I have spent more than forty years in the financial market, including time at India's largest bank and leading financial institutions in Bahrain. Managing forex activities was an important part of my long career. Therefore, in this book, I have tried to impart the knowledge and experience I have gained to date.

Anyone who hopes to pursue a career in foreign exchange, banking, or the financial arena should have first-hand knowledge of foreign exchange and the intricacies involved in it. Further, a deeper study of the subject is needed in order to build a successful career in currency trading. This book is a great first step for someone with those aspirations.

This book starts with an introduction to foreign exchange and takes you through the major participants in the market, the factors affecting exchange rates, exchange rate arithmetic, currency hedging, derivative instruments (such as currency options and futures), and various exchange rate regimes. In addition, the book gives you a historical perspective of the foreign exchange market and discusses various currency crises that have occurred since the floating exchange rate system came into effect. Finally, the book provides an overview of world currencies, including some very useful and specific data. The public data from various central banks and financial entities were vital for the creation of this book, and I have shared a great deal of that information.

The book is a good resource for students of finance, investment analysts, newcomers to the foreign exchange profession, and portfolio managers engaged in global investment management. Further, this book is a good resource for universities and financial institutions.

My former secretary, Philomena, and my daughter, Jenny, deserve my special gratitude and thanks for their assistance during the production of this book. Also, this book would not have seen the light of day without the encouragement from my wife, Julie.

The contents of this book are not intended to provide recommendations for currency trading. Anybody wishing to perform foreign exchange transactions is encouraged to do the required research and risk/reward analysis to gauge the suitability of such actions.

I wish you a fruitful reading experience.

Chapter 1

An Introduction to Foreign Exchange

Definition of foreign exchange

Foreign exchange is defined as the conversion of one currency into another currency. In other words, it is the exchange of one currency for another. The term *foreign exchange* is also known as *forex, FX,* or *currency.*

Foreign exchange market: an overview

The foreign exchange market (forex market) refers to the market in which various participants buy and sell currencies. The forex market is very decentralised. The various participants in the forex market include central banks, banks, financial institutions, sovereign wealth funds, commercial companies, investment firms, hedge funds, forex brokers, and individual investors. The forex market operates around the clock, with the exception of weekends. There are a number of platforms for trading forex. Reuters, Bloomberg, and EBS are the key trading platforms. In addition, there are several smaller platforms that allow individual investors to trade forex. Such platforms have mushroomed in recent years. In terms of volume, the global foreign exchange market is, by far, the largest financial market—the average daily volume is counted in trillions of dollars. The Bank for International Settlements (BIS) estimates that the daily average foreign exchange turnover is close to five trillion USD, which consists of spot transactions, outright forwards, foreign exchange swaps, and derivatives (including options and futures).

The foreign exchange market has certain unique characteristics, as follows:

- The FX market is truly global in nature.
- It operates continuously in multiple time zones (twenty-four hours per day except weekends).
- The market is highly liquid, and the trading volume is huge.
- It operates at a very low trading margin (bid-offer spread) compared to other asset classes.
- The market reacts instantly to any information, including economic and monetary data releases.
- There is no restriction in going long or short (i.e., there is no uptick rule).
- Leverage is used to enhance profit.
- There is no centralised exchange to trade forex.
- It is a global, decentralised, over-the-counter financial market.

Evolution of the modern foreign exchange market

The development of the modern foreign exchange market began during the 1970s, when countries abandoned the fixed exchange rate system governed by the Bretton Woods Agreement and adopted floating exchange rates. The foreign exchange market assists international trade and investments by facilitating currency conversions. The sharp rise in oil prices in the 1970s and early 1980s created heavy demand for US dollars because oil prices were denominated in US dollars. This situation pushed up the volume in the foreign exchange market as oil importing countries rushed to exchange their domestic currencies for US dollars to pay for their oil imports. The advancement in globalisation and the substantial rise in world trade was another contributing factor for the rise in forex trading volume. The migration of labour, to the Middle East, mainly—and the resultant increase in global remittances—also added to the rise in forex trading in subsequent years. The volume of forex trading rose almost eight times during the twenty-one year period from 1989 to 2010. The turnover increased from five hundred billion dollars in 1989 to almost four trillion in 2010.

The introduction of the euro on 1 January 1999 reduced the number of currencies traded on the foreign exchange market. Still, the market turnover is on the rise despite the seasonal declines in volume traded. One of the important characteristics of the foreign exchange market is the rise in its volatility. This phenomenon is the result of the interplay between currency speculators and the coordinated central bank interventions in the market to halt excessive currency movement. The price actions in certain key commodities, such as oil and gold, in recent years have also impacted the volatility in the foreign exchange market.

The foreign exchange market, which was once accessible only to large banks, financial institutions, and corporations, is now within reach for individuals due to the advent of internet trading and the existence of several smaller currency trading platforms. Factors that have contributed to the retail participation in the foreign exchange market include the ease of access, the ability to trade twenty-four hours per day and five days per week, high liquidity, low margin requirements, narrow bid-offer spreads, and general volatility in the market.

Chapter 2

Foreign Exchange Market—Major Participants

Overview

There are several participants in the foreign exchange market, but the market has different levels of access for different types of market participants. The interbank foreign exchange market (interbank market) is at the top of the ladder. The interbank market consists mainly of the largest commercial banks. The interbank market trades currencies at the tightest spreads due to the large volumes traded. The bid-ask spread widens as one heads down the access ladder. The volume of the trade is a key determinant of the bid-offer spread. In fact, the interbank market accounts for a significant portion of the total volume traded in the foreign exchange market. The other players on the access ladder are smaller banks, multinational companies, sovereign wealth funds, asset managers, hedge funds, exchange houses, and retail players. The retail players receive the least favourable bid-offers. Central banks participate in the foreign exchange market to implement their monetary policies and influence exchange rates as part of their market actions. At times, several central banks participate in coordinated interventions in the foreign exchange market to prevent excessive currency fluctuations and bring stability to the market.

A discussion about the key market participants follows:

Interbank market

As the prefix suggests, the interbank market is between banks. The term refers to the currency market in which the largest banks transact currency trades among themselves. They trade currencies in large volumes, either for themselves or for their customers. Because of the competition among banks, the pricing in the interbank market is fair and trades take place at tight bid-offer spreads. Transactions in the interbank market constitute a large part of the total volume in the foreign exchange market. The interbank market is currently concentrated in the hands of a small number of major global banks or financial institutions, such as Citigroup, JP Morgan Chase, Goldman Sachs, Deutsche Bank, UBS, Barclays, and Royal Bank of Scotland. There are hundreds of other international banks and financial institutions trading alongside the major banks. The interbank market operates without any significant governmental controls or regulations.

Central banks

Central banks play a crucial role in the foreign exchange market. They intervene in the foreign exchange market in order to control the money supply, domestic interest rates, inflationary level in the country, exchange rate of their currencies, and volatility to the market. Any such operations will have an effect on the reserves of the country. The timing of central bank interventions is quite unpredictable. In times of extreme currency volatility, several central banks carry out joint interventions in the foreign exchange market with a view to controlling excessive volatility.

Multinational firms

Multinational firms are domestic firms engaged in business with foreign countries. They have to deal in the foreign exchange market to buy or sell foreign currencies as part of their daily business. They need to buy foreign currencies to pay for their imports, and they need to sell foreign currencies to exchange export proceeds for their national currencies. In addition, multinational companies use the foreign exchange market to hedge their currency risk.

Sovereign wealth funds

Sovereign wealth funds (SWFs) are state-owned investment funds that invest a state's surpluses domestically or internationally. SWFs have been major players in the global financial market for years, but their role has assumed a new proportion in the wake of the 2008 financial crisis. Ultimately, SWFs came to the rescue of several global financial institutions and lifted them out of bankruptcy. Their international investments are large, involving significant amount of foreign exchange transactions. Hence, SWFs play an important role in the foreign exchange market.

Asset managers

Asset Managers (aka investment management firms) manage significant amounts in international markets on behalf of SWFs, pension funds, endowments, and others. They use the foreign exchange market to facilitate their transactions in foreign securities. They also have currency specialists who manage their clients' currency exposures with a view to generating profits and limiting currency risks. As a result, asset managers handle large currency transactions.

Hedge funds/speculators

Hedge funds are also major players in the foreign exchange market. They trade in the foreign exchange market for speculative purposes to generate returns for their investors over and above the average market return. Most forex hedge funds are trend followers, meaning they tend to build long-term currency positions to profit from long-term uptrends or downtrends in the market. Hedge funds have also earned a reputation for aggressive currency speculation in the past. An example is George Soros's Quantum fund, which made a very large amount of money by betting against the Bank of England in 1992. Soros also earned a significant amount in a couple of months by shorting the Japanese yen in 2013. There are cases in which speculators have brought down institutions along with themselves because the speculations resulted in huge losses. Nick Leeson's story provides a great example. As a derivatives trader at Barings Bank, he took speculative positions in yen futures that resulted in losses of more than 1.4 billion USD, which led to the collapse of the centuries-old bank in 1995. Whereas speculators contribute to liquidity and market activity, speculative currency trading involves huge risks as seen in the previous example.

Exchange houses (bureau de change)

Exchange houses are small players in the foreign exchange market. They make money mainly from the difference in the buying and selling rates, which are normally wider than those quoted by banks. They also earn commission on their services, such as money transfers. Tourists make use of exchange houses to exchange one currency for another.

Retail foreign exchange traders

The growth in the retail foreign exchange platforms has made retail currency traders a small segment of the market. They participate in the market through banks or retail brokers. Retail brokers also form part of this segment of participants.

Chapter 3

Factors Affecting Exchange Rates

Overview

In a fixed exchange rate regime, a country's government or central bank ties the exchange rate of its currency to another country's currency. In a floating exchange rate regime, rates are determined by various market factors that affect the currency. Currency fluctuations are a natural outcome of the floating exchange rate system. Most of the major economies have adopted the floating exchange rate regime. In the shorter timeframe, anything can influence the exchange rate. In the past, events such as the health of a country's leader, the threat of war, and terrorist attacks have affected exchange rates (but such impacts were short-lived). But on a broader level, there are several factors that influence the exchange rate of a currency. A discussion of those factors follows.

Theoretical exchange rates

There are various models (such as purchasing power parity, balance of payment, and interest rate parity) used to determine the theoretical exchange rates. Of course, a detailed discussion of such models exceeds the scope of this book.

Key factors affecting exchange rates

There are various fundamental and technical factors that influence exchange rates. Such factors include the relative supply and demand of the two currencies in the currency pair, interest rate differentials between the two countries, inflation differentials, economic fundamentals, capital flows, and technical factors.

Fundamental factors

The fundamental factors that influence exchange rates can be broadly divided into the following three categories:

- Economic factors

- Political factors

- Market factors

A brief discussion of the above factors is provided here:

Economic factors

- **Economic policy:** The economic policy of a country, as reflected in its fiscal and monetary policies, impacts the level of interest rates in the country, and in turn, its exchange rate. The periodical release of economic data (such as employment data, industrial production data, reports from monetary authorities, and information about investment fund flows) from a country are likely to cause fluctuations in the exchange rate of that country.

- **Fiscal policy:** A country's fiscal policy affects its spending, tax rates, and public deficit. A country with high debt is not favoured as an investment destination by foreigners. The level of public debt held by a country—and the mode by which such deficits are financed— may adversely affect the debt rating of the country, and in turn, its currency.

- **Monetary policy:** The monetary policy of a country is a key factor in determining the appreciation and depreciation of its currency. Changes in a country's monetary policy from time to time will be reflected in the exchange rate of its currency. A country pursuing an easy monetary policy will increase the supply of its currency, which will cause its currency to depreciate. On the other hand, a country pursuing a restrictive monetary policy will decrease the supply of its currency, which will cause its currency to appreciate.

If a country's central bank is pursuing an restrictive monetary policy while its trading partner is pursuing a much easier policy, the former country's currency will be relatively stronger than that of the latter.

- **Inflation:** The level of inflation prevailing within a country affects its currency. Typically, high or rising inflation will erode the purchasing power of the currency, pushing the exchange rate lower.

- **Current account:** The current account deficit (or surplus) of a country is a reflection of its economic performance. Trade deficits occur when a country's economy is growing faster than the economy of its trading partner. Strong economic growth increases the demand for imports, which creates demand for foreign currencies to pay for the imports. This situation will likely result in the depreciation of that country's currency. The capital flows into a country that offers investment opportunities will tend to push up the value of that country's currency.

- **Interest rates:** High interest rates in a country will result in the inflow of "hot" money, which will create demand for that currency. The inflow of capital over the last few years into emerging market bonds with high interest rates (against the background of low interest rates in leading economies) is worth noting. The demand thus created for the currency will push up the value of that nation's currency.

Political factors

- A country with political stability will attract foreign investments and improve investor confidence in the country. This is positive for the currency of the country.

- Political instability may negatively affect a country's currency because foreign investors are likely to desert the country.

Market factors

* Market speculation is another factor that influences exchange rates. One financial adage—buy on rumour, sell on fact—holds true here. When the market expects that a particular currency will appreciate, it will generate a buying frenzy. On the contrary, if the market speculates that a currency is likely to depreciate, investors will start selling that currency, which will push the currency lower.

* Certain global events not directly related to a country can impact that country's currency. A good example is the turmoil in the global currency market that happened on 20 June 2013, following the announcement by the US Federal Reserve that it might cut back on its bond buying programme in the near future, a measure known as quantitative easing (QE).

Technical factors

In addition to fundamental factors, technical factors also influence exchange rates. There are various technical tools used to forecast exchange rate trends. Though all the fundamental factors discussed thus far are taken into consideration by technical analysts, there are certain common indicators used in the technical analysis. These indicators are as follows:

* Moving averages

* Moving average convergence divergence (MACD)

* Support levels

* Resistance levels

* Bolinger bands

* Stochastics

* Fibonacci retracements

Chapter 4

Exchange Rate Arithmetic

Exchange rate quotations

In order to get a handle on how exchange rates are quoted, a good understanding of currency pairs, bid-offers, direct quotes, indirect quotes, spot rates, and forward rates is needed.

Currency pair

In the foreign exchange market, exchange rate is quoted in terms of a currency pair. A currency pair is the quotation of a base currency against a term currency. The base currency is also called the unit currency, and the term *currency* is also known as price currency. Thus, the quotation EUR/USD:1.3000 means that 1 euro is exchanged for 1.30 US dollars. In this quotation, EUR is called the base currency or unit currency, and USD is called the term currency or price currency.

The foreign exchange market follows certain market conventions when quoting currency pairs. The market convention determines which is the base currency and which is the term currency. The following seven currency pairs are the major ones in the foreign exchange market:

- EUR/USD
- GBP/USD
- USD/CHF
- USD/JPY
- AUD/USD
- NZD/USD
- USD/CAD

Among the above currency pairs, the most liquid and widely traded currency pairs are EUR/USD, USD/JPY, GBP/USD, and USD/CHF, in that order. The other three currency pairs are known as "commodity currency pairs" because AUD, NZD, and CAD are from countries that possess large quantities of commodities and/or natural resources. All seven pairs include the US dollar as one of the traded currencies. It may be noted that a significant part of the daily foreign exchange transactions involves the US dollar.

Bid-offer

In a foreign exchange quote, one side is the bid and the other side is the offer. The bid is the price at which the foreign exchange dealer is willing to buy the currency; the offer side is the price at which the dealer is willing to sell the currency. For example, if a dealer is quoting USD/JPY as 100.05/100.07, the first quote is the bid (the price at which the dealer is willing to buy US dollars against Japanese yen) and the second quote is the offer (the price at which the dealer is willing to sell US dollars against Japanese yen). This means that, if you want to buy yen and sell dollars, the dealer would give you 100.05 yen per dollar. If you want to buy dollars and sell yen, the dealer would take 100.07 yen per dollar. The difference between the bid and the offer is called the spread. The spread represents the cost of transacting a currency. The bid-offer spread is a function of various market factors, mainly the supply/demand for the currencies in the pair.

Percentage in point (pip)

Pip refers to the minimum fluctuation of an exchange rate. A pip is equal to 1/100th of 1 per cent. Most of the currency pairs (except Japanese yen) are quoted to four decimal places. For those currencies, a pip means one unit of the fourth decimal point. In the case of the yen, a pip means one unit of the second decimal point. In the case of the US dollar, euro, British pound, or Swiss franc, one pip is about 0.0001. In the case of Japanese yen, one pip is about 0.01.

Direct quote

In the foreign exchange market, a direct quote is equal to the number of domestic currency per unit of the foreign currency. In this case, the foreign currency is fixed at one unit and the domestic currency varies. For example, for Japanese yen, the quote in Japan might be as follows: 1 USD = JPY 100.00

Indirect quote

In an indirect quote, the foreign currency is the variable; the domestic currency is fixed at one unit. For example, for the euro, the quote in Europe might be 1 EUR = USD 1.3000.

Spot exchange rate

Spot exchange rate (aka spot rate) is the rate of a foreign exchange contract for immediate delivery. In other words, it is the current exchange rate at which a currency can be bought or sold. In the FX spot market, the delivery of a currency takes place within two days from the trade date. Spot trades are done on a T+2 settlement basis; i.e., settlement two days after the trade date. However, the settlement date will be extended to the next market day if there are any holidays in the countries of the currency pair or if there is a weekend that falls in between the trade and settlement days.

Forward exchange rate

Forward exchange rate (aka forward rate) is the rate of a foreign exchange contract for future delivery. Under normal market conditions, the forward rate is determined by the spot rate. It is also determined by the difference between the interest rates for the forward period between the two currencies involved and the dealers' margin. However, there are other factors that may impact the forward rates. Events such as government intervention in the currency market or any situation that affects the currencies in the pair can influence the forward rate. The forward rate will be at a discount or premium to the spot rate, depending on the difference in interest rates between the currencies involved. The determination of the theoretical forward rate is explained using the following equation:

Where:

> S = The current spot exchange rate
> F = The forward exchange rate
> i_d = The interest rate in the domestic currency for the period to delivery
> i_f = The interest rate in the foreign currency for the period to delivery

The forward rate is determined using the following equation:

$$F = \frac{S \, (1+i_d)}{(1+i_f)}$$

The forward rate can also be determined based on the premium or discount, using the following equation:

$$F = S \, (1+P)$$

Where

F = Forward rate
S = Spot rate
P = The premium (if positive) or the discount (if negative)

Care should be taken to calculate the premium or discount for the actual period to delivery if the dealers quote the premium or discount as an annualised percentage of the spot rate.

The forward premium or discount is illustrated in the following example:

If the three-month USD/JPY forward exchange rate is 100.50, and the spot exchange rate for USD/JPY is 100.40, the dollar is at a premium of 0.10 yen per dollar. In other words, the yen would be at a discount because the forward value of yen in terms of the dollar is less than its spot rate.

Long/short currency position

To long (aka long position) a currency means buying that currency with the expectation that the currency will rise in value. To short (aka short position) a currency means selling a currency with the expectation that the currency will fall in value. In a currency pair transaction, one side is a long position and the other side is a short position. For example, if an investor purchases USD by selling JPY, the investor is long USD and short JPY.

Cross rate

Cross rate refers to the foreign exchange rate between two currencies other than the US dollar. For example, the cross rate of euro for yen might be based on the rate of euro for dollar and dollar for yen. There are both spot and forward cross rates. Here's an example that illustrates how to calculate a spot cross rate:

Spot EUR/JPY cross rate:

If:

1 EUR = USD 1.3200
1 USD = JPY 98.1000

Then:

1 EUR = 1.3200 * 98.1000
= JPY 129.4920

Thus, 1 euro is equal to 129.4920 yen.

In market parlance, the bank (foreign exchange dealer) quotes bid-ask spread for a currency pair. With bid-ask spread, the calculation of cross rate becomes complex. An example of a cross rate calculation using bid-ask spread follows:

Spot EUR/JPY cross rate with bid-ask spread:

Quotes from the bank for:

EUR/USD: 1.3195/1.3200
USD/JPY: 98.10/98.15

From the above quotation, cross rate between EUR/JPY can be calculated as follows:

- Bank buys 1 EUR and pays 1.3195 USD
- Bank sells 1 EUR and receives 1.3200 USD
- Bank buys 1 USD and pays 98.10 JPY
- Bank sells 1 USD and receives 98.15 JPY

To arrive at the bid rate for EUR/JPY (EUR as the base currency and JPY as the quote currency), the bank must sell JPY and buy EUR. There are two steps to achieve this goal:

- The bank must sell JPY and buy USD
- Simultaneously, the bank must sell USD and buy EUR.

Thus:

1 EUR = 1.3195 USD and 1 USD = 98.10 JPY, or
1 EUR = 1.3195 x 98.10 = 129.443 JPY.

Thus, the bank's bid for 1 EUR will be at 129.443 JPY.

To arrive at the ask rate for EUR/JPY (EUR as the base currency and JPY as the quote currency), the bank must buy JPY and sell EUR. This is achieved in two steps, as follows:

- The bank must buy JPY and sell USD.
- Simultaneously, the bank must buy USD and sell EUR.

Thus:

1 EUR = 1.3200 USD and 1 USD = 98.15 JPY, or
1 EUR = 1.3200 x 98.15 = 129.558 JPY.

Thus, the bank's offer for 1 EUR will be at 129.558 JPY.

Hence, the cross rate for EUR/JPY is as follows: Bid 129.443/Ask 129.558

Forward cross rates

Cross rates for different currency pairs for different maturities can be found out in a similar manner as the spot cross rates were deduced. While calculating cross rates, take care to employ appropriate methods for quoting rates.

Comments

The computations for cross rates are not as complex as they look because cross rates for most currency pairs are readily available in all major trading platforms/market information systems (such as Reuters and Bloomberg). Quotes given by banks can be compared with rates from the trading platforms to verify correctness. But bear in mind that quotes from banks to retail customers may not be the same as the interbank rates shown on the trading platforms, which is due to the amount of the transaction, the bank's margin, etc.

Forex arbitrage

The foreign exchange market provides arbitrage opportunities due to pricing inefficiencies. The objective of forex arbitrage is to profit from inefficiencies in the market that are present only for a short period of time. Because traders will spot such opportunities as they arise, arbitrage opportunities disappear quickly. Still, it is a risk-free strategy to profit without having any open currency exposure. The strategy involves buying and selling different currency pairs to exploit the pricing inefficiencies.

Example of forex arbitrage

Assume three currency pairs are quoted as follows:

EUR/USD: 1.3275
EUR/GBP: 0.8635
GBP/USD: 1.5385

A forex trader could buy 10,000 euros for 13,275 US dollars. He could sell the euros and buy 8,635 British pounds, which he could then sell for 13,285 US dollars. In that case, he would make a profit of 10 US dollars. There is no currency exposure involved because long positions cancel short positions in each currency. Remember: a trader must act quickly to capture such arbitrage opportunities.

Chapter 5

Exchange Rate Regimes

Introduction

Since the abolition of the fixed exchange rate system in 1971, several countries adopted the floating exchange rate regime. However, many countries have yet to take on the new system. What follows are the preconditions to facilitate a transition to the floating exchange rate regime:

- Creation of a liquid foreign exchange market
- A clear central bank policy to handle intervention in the foreign exchange market
- Enough reserves to intervene in the forex market
- An effective system for managing the currency risk
- Interest rate liberalisation
- Favourable economic factors

As more countries accomplish the above conditions, we could see the floating exchange rate system becoming even more prevalent, leading to further growth in the global foreign exchange market.

Types of exchange rate arrangements

The various exchange rate arrangements prevalent currently are as follows:

- Fixed-peg
- Floating exchange rate
- Managed float
- No separate legal tender

- Currency board
- Stabilised
- Crawling peg
- Crawl-like
- Pegged exchange rate within horizontal bands
- Dollarisation
- Other managed system

All currencies operate in one of the aforementioned arrangements. A brief explanation of each follows:

Fixed-peg

In a fixed-peg exchange rate (fixed exchange rate) system, a country pegs its currency at a fixed rate to another currency or a basket of currencies of the country's main trading partners. The country may also choose a commodity, such as gold, for this purpose. The central bank remains committed to buying and selling its currency at a fixed exchange rate. The central bank provides foreign currencies to meet imbalances in the balance of payments.

Floating exchange rate

A country's exchange rate regime that keeps the value of its currency open to the forces of supply and demand in the foreign exchange market. Currently, a large part of the world's currencies are floating. However, the central banks of those countries intervene in the currency markets at times to influence their exchange rates. Occasionally, there are coordinated interventions in highly volatile markets to bring stability to the markets.

Managed float

A floating exchange rate in which the government intervenes at times to influence the direction of its currency's exchange rate (by buying or selling the currency). There may be situations in which one country intervenes in another country's exchange rate. In 1994, during the Mexican financial crisis, the US government intervened in the currency market by buying large quantities of Mexican pesos to protect the value from plunging. Such action not only helped stabilise the peso, it also helped it recoup a good part of the losses.

No separate legal tender

The situation in which one country accepts other countries' currency as legal tender. This may result in the central bank of one country yielding its independence to another country.

Currency board

The currency board is a country's monetary authority that issues notes and coins, but it doesn't act as the lender of last resort. In most cases, the currency board is an entity separate from a country's central bank.

Stabilised arrangement

An arrangement involving a spot market exchange rate that remains within a margin of 2 per cent for six months or more and is not floating. The margin of stability is decided against a single currency or basket of currencies. In order to select the single currency or basket of currencies for the margin of stability, statistical methods may be used.

Crawling peg

In a crawling peg arrangement, a currency with a fixed exchange rate is adjusted in small amounts or in response to changes in market factors, such as inflation. The rate of crawl is based on a predetermined, fixed rate. Alternatively, the rate is based on the inflation-adjusted changes in the exchange rate.

Crawl-like arrangement

In a crawl-like arrangement, the exchange rate must remain within a narrow margin of 2 per cent relative to a statistically identified trend for six months or more. Plus, the exchange rate arrangement cannot be considered floating. Usually, in this arrangement, a minimum rate of change greater than allowed under a stabilised arrangement is required.

Pegged exchange rate within horizontal bands

Under this arrangement, the value of the currency is maintained within certain margins of fluctuation—at least +/—1 per cent around a fixed central rate. Alternatively, the currency's margin must stay between the maximum and minimum value of the exchange rate that exceeds 2 per cent.

Dollarisation

Under this regime, the inhabitants of a country use a foreign currency instead of the domestic currency (or in parallel with the domestic currency). The term is applicable to any foreign currency; it's not confined to the usage of US dollars.

Other managed arrangements

This category is used when the exchange rate arrangement does not meet the criteria for any other categories.

Chapter 6

Currency Hedging

Definition

Currency hedging (also known as forex hedging) is defined as the strategy used to reduce the risks in the foreign exchange market. In other words, it is a transaction used to protect a currency position from an adverse movement in the currency's exchange rate. Thus, a long position in a currency pair can be protected from downside risk and a short position in a currency pair can be protected from upside risk.

Foreign exchange risk

Foreign exchange risk exists where currency exposure exists. Foreign exchange risk is the risk that an exchange rate will move adversely before the currency is exchanged. When companies conduct business across borders, they must deal in foreign currencies. This reality gives rise to foreign exchange risk: companies must exchange home currencies for foreign currencies in order to pay for imports. An export company also runs the risk of foreign exchange when it exchanges foreign currency export proceeds for home currency.

Hedging currency risk

An investor can react to foreign exchange risk in two ways. The first option is to do nothing. This decision forces the investor to accept the foreign exchange risk, including any losses that may result from the currency exposure. The second option is to hedge the risk by shifting some or all of the exchange risk to others. The decision to hedge or not is complex. The choice depends upon how much volatility the investor is exposed to, how much volatility can be reduced, and the cost of the hedge. There are three typical hedge options for investors who decide to mitigate foreign exchange exposure. These choices are as follows:

- Symmetrical hedge

- Asymmetrical hedge

- Active currency management

• **Symmetrical hedge:** In a symmetrical hedging strategy, currency forwards or futures are used. This type of hedge can be used as a *matched hedge* or a *basket hedge.* In a matched hedge, the investor uses the same currency he or she is exposed to in order to hedge the foreign exchange exposure. The hedged return on a fully hedged asset position mirrors the local asset return, minus the cost of hedge. A basket hedge uses a mix of currencies to create a symmetrical hedge similar to a matched hedge. The purpose of a basket hedge is to use the natural correlations between specific currencies to construct a statistical proxy for the fully hedged position. A basket hedge is worthwhile only if the cost of hedge is cheaper than a full hedge. The disadvantage of a basket hedge is that the currencies in the basket may behave differently than expected. Further, the hedge may not be effective if the correlations between the currencies in question do not remain stable. An investor has to weigh all options before undertaking a basket hedge.

• **Asymmetrical hedge:** This hedging strategy involves the use of foreign exchange options or strategies that replicate options. The two most common strategies used are the *protective put* and the *range forward (collar).* The protective put strategy is implemented through the purchase of currency put options, with the strike price set at the desired level of protection for the period of hedge. Purchasing the put option provides the investor with downside protection if the currency moves downward, and it leaves the investor with the upside potential if the currency moves upward. But the cost of the option reduces the full return to some extent. The range forward (collar) hedge is carried out by selling a call option in addition to buying a put option. The maturity of the call option matches the maturity of the put option, but the strike price of the call option is set at a higher level than the put's strike price. The premium received from the sale of the call option will offset the cost of the put option to some extent, but the investor will not benefit if the currency appreciates beyond the call's strike price.

• **Active currency management:** Active currency management strategies offer the opportunity to enhance the return and reduce the downside risk. There are several ways to pursue active currency management. The most common ways are as follows:

- Fundamental

- Technical

- Dynamic

- Option-based

Fundamental approaches use economic and fundamental data to manage currency exposure. Technical approaches use price history and price trends. Dynamic strategy uses currency forwards or option technology to generate profits and to limit losses. Option-based strategies make use of systematic differences between implied and actual future volatility of currencies. A deeper analysis of the active currency management is beyond the scope of this book.

Chapter 7

Currency Codes

Introduction

Currencies are represented via internationally accepted currency codes. The three-letter alphabetic codes issued by the International Organisation for Standardisation (ISO) are the globally accepted currency codes. ISO 4217 is the international standard for currency codes. The ISO currency code standards are periodically updated and published. As of the writing of this book, ISO 4217:2008 is the most recent edition of the standard. In addition to the alphabetic codes, currencies can be represented by three-digit numeric codes.

Alphabetic codes

In the three-letter alphabetic code, the first two letters are the same as the code for the country name, as stated in ISO 3166. The third letter corresponds to the first letter of the currency name.

For example:

- The US dollar is represented as *USD*. The *U* and *S* denote the country code of the United States (as per ISO 3166), and the *D* stands for *dollar.*

- The Japanese yen is represented as *JPY.* The *J* and *P* denote the country code (as per ISO 3166), and the *Y* stands for *yen.*

- The Indian Rupee is represented as *INR.* The *I* and *N* denotes the country code (as per ISO 3166), and the *R* stands for *rupee.*

The alphabetic codes are widely used by foreign exchange dealers, the Bank for International Settlement (BIS), commercial banks, exchange bureaus, travel agencies, airlines, and the media.

Numeric codes

The three-digit numeric codes for currencies issued by ISO 4217 are used in computer systems and in countries that do not use Latin scripts.

The three-letter alphabetic and numeric currency codes for various currencies are shown in Chapter 13.

Currency symbols

Although currency codes are used internationally for official purposes, most currencies can be represented by shorthand symbols. Currency symbols are used mostly domestically.

What follows are some of the popular currency symbols:

Currency	Symbol
US dollar	$
Euro	€
Pound sterling	£
Japanese yen	¥

Chapter 8

Currency Options

Introduction

A currency option is a derivative financial instrument. It is used as a vehicle to hedge foreign exchange risk. This chapter discusses the basics of currency options.

Definition of currency option

A currency option is a contract that grants the holder of the option the right—but not the obligation—to buy or sell a currency at an agreed-upon exchange rate during a specified period of time. An option that gives the holder the right to buy is called a call option, and an option that gives the holder the right to sell is called a put option.

Options nomenclature

- **Option holder:** The option holder is the person who buys the right conveyed by the option.

- **Option writer:** The option writer is the person who sells the currency option. The option writer is obligated—if and when the option is assigned—to perform according to the terms of the option.

- **Exercise price:** The exercise price is the price at which the option holder has the right to either buy or sell the underlying currency. It is also called the strike price.

- **Expiration date:** The expiration date is the date on which the currency option expires. If an option is not exercised prior to its expiration, it ceases to exist.

- **Option style:** The option style refers to the time when an option is exercisable. Though there are several styles, there are two styles widely used in the currency option market: American-style and European-style. An American-style option is exercisable at any time prior to its expiration. A European-style option is exercisable only during a specified period before the option expires (or only on the expiration date).

- **Exercise:** An exercise is a notice. In order to exercise an option, the option holder must give an exercise notice to the option seller, as per applicable procedures. The notice is sent to the option writer stating that the option sold has been exercised by the purchaser of the option. It is also known as an assignment.

- **Option premium:** The option premium is the price that the holder of a currency option pays and the writer of the option receives for the rights conveyed by the option. The option premium is decided by a combination of factors, including the intrinsic value, the time value, and the implied volatility of the underlying asset. The time value decays as the option approaches its expiry.

- **Opening transaction:** An opening transaction refers to the purchase or sale transaction through which an option is established.

- **Closing transaction:** A closing transaction occurs at some point prior to expiration, when the option holder makes an offsetting sale of an identical option (or the option writer makes an offsetting purchase of an identical option).

- **Long/short:** Long and short are two different positions an investor can take. *Long* refers to a person's position as the holder of an option, and *short* refers to a person's position as the writer of an option.

- **At the money:** At the money is a term that means that the exercise price of an option is the same as the current exchange rate.

- **In the money:** In the money is a term used when the exercise price of a call option is below the current exchange rate. A put option is said to be in the money when the current exchange rate is below the exercise price of the option.

- **Out of the money:** Out of the money is a term used when the exercise price of a call option is above the current exchange rate. Likewise, if the current exchange rate is above the exercise price of a put option, the option is said to be out of the money.

Foreign exchange options market

The foreign exchange options market is one of the largest markets in terms of volume. Only a small percentage is traded in stock exchanges (such as the Philadelphia Stock Exchange, the Chicago Mercantile Exchange, and the International Securities Exchange); most of the trading takes place over-the-counter (OTC). Whereas trading on stock exchanges is highly regulated, trading on the OTC market is less regulated. Options traded on stock exchanges are standardised, but OTC options can be tailored to the investor's requirements. In addition to the above platforms, online forex trading platforms are offered by several institutions.

Example of a currency option

Imagine an option contract EUR/USD gives the option holder the right to sell euros (e.g., EUR 1,000,000) and buy dollars (e.g., USD 1,300,000) at an exchange rate of 1.30 dollars per euro, on an agreed date (e.g., December 30th.)

In this example, the notional amounts of the option contract are EUR 1,000,000 and USD 1,300,000. The strike price is 1 EUR = 1.30 USD. The exercise or assignment date is December 30th. The contract is both a call on US dollar and a put on euro. In other words, it is a EUR/USD put and a USD/EUR call.

If the spot rate on December 30th is 1.2500, this means that the euro is weaker and the dollar is stronger compared to the time when the option was opened. In this case, the option will be exercised (because the put is in the money), which allows the owner to sell EUR 1,000,000 at 1.30 dollars per euro and receive USD 1,300,000. Because the spot rate is below, the investor could immediately buy the euro in the market at 1.25 dollars (i.e., he or she could buy EUR 1,000,000 and pay USD 1,250,000 and make a profit of USD 50,000). If the investor converts the profit of USD 50,000 immediately into EUR, this will amount to EUR 40,000 (USD 50,000/1.25 = EUR 40,000).

Chapter 9

Currency Futures

Definition

Currency futures are exchange-traded contracts to exchange one currency for another at an agreed-upon rate on a specified date in the future. The rate is agreed-upon when the contract is initiated. One of the currencies involved is typically the US dollar. All futures contracts have a specific termination (expiry) date. Unless an offsetting trade is made on the initial position, the futures contract requires delivery of the currency on the termination date.

Forex futures: further explanation

Currency futures are also known as:

- FX futures
- Foreign exchange futures
- Forex futures

Futures contracts serve mainly two purposes:

- Investors use forex futures to hedge currency risk.

- Speculators use futures contracts to profit from the direction of a currency.

Hedging

Investors use forex futures contracts to hedge their exposure in a currency. For example, an exporting company receiving export proceeds in a foreign currency is exposed to currency risk until the foreign currency is converted into the domestic currency. Such a company may utilise the futures market to hedge the currency risk.

Speculation

Speculators use the forex futures market to speculate on the direction of a currency to profit from its fluctuation. For example, a speculator expecting a currency to appreciate may go long on the futures contract for that currency.

More on the futures

Because currency futures are traded in exchanges, they are highly regulated. Exchanges provide centralised pricing and clearing. Irrespective of the broker being used for a futures trade, the market price will be roughly the same. Currency futures are traded on several exchanges in the United States and abroad. A significant percentage of currency futures is traded on the Chicago Mercantile Exchange (CME) through its partner brokers. Futures contracts are standardised in terms of the contract size and the delivery date. The delivery date (maturity date) falls on the third Wednesday of March, June, September, and December. Currency futures are settled in cash in the underlying currency on the delivery date. However, investors can close out a position prior to the delivery date. In addition to CME, forex futures are traded on other exchanges such as Euronext, Liffe, Tokyo Stock Exchange, and Intercontinental Exchange.

There are margin requirements applicable to currency futures. A participant has to pay an initial margin at the time the contract is established. Futures positions are marked to the market on a daily basis. Hence, in addition to the initial margin, a holder has to meet the maintenance margin. Margin calls are made on a daily basis. When marking to the market a futures position, the profit or loss is calculated.

Before entering into a forex futures contract, an investor needs to look at the pros and cons by comparing the benefits of futures with other alternatives such as forward contracts.

Chapter 10

Currency Market—A Historical Perspective

Introduction

It is useful to look at the market's history to understand how the global foreign exchange market has performed over the past several years. The year 1971 can be considered the birth year of the free-floating foreign exchange market because many countries decided to float their currencies when the Bretton Woods system was dismantled on 15 August 1971. That dismantling put an end to the fixed currency regime. The performance of the foreign exchange market since then has been interesting. The volume traded in the FX market has grown consistently. Today, the FX market is the largest market among all asset classes. In order to look at the performance of the market, I have included an analysis of the US dollar index (known as the DXY index), which was created in 1973.

Currency returns

Investment in currency offers two sources of return to the investor: the carry, which is the difference between the interest rates of the two currencies in a currency pair; and the fluctuations in exchange rates. The fluctuations in exchange rates are caused by several factors, such as changes in relative interest rates, economic events, political events, and international events. These factors are subject to change. Currency returns have exhibited a low correlation with the returns of other asset classes historically; hence, adding a currency component to a portfolio may provide diversification benefits to the investor.

36

The US dollar index (DXY index)

The US dollar index (DXY index) is the most widely recognised benchmark for the value of the US dollar. The index was introduced in 1973, following the abrogation of the Bretton Woods system. The index measures the movement of the US dollar against a basket of currencies. The currencies in the basket are some of the major trading partners of the United States. Initially, the basket had ten currencies, but as of the writing of this book, there are six: euro, Japanese yen, pound sterling, Canadian dollar, Swedish krona, and Swiss franc. The component currencies were altered only once, when the euro was introduced in January of 1999. The euro replaced the German mark, French franc, Italian lira, Dutch guilder, and Belgian franc as it came into the basket.

The component currencies do not have the same weight in the index. The current weightings of the component currencies in the DXY index are as follows:

DXY index weightings

Currency	Weight (percentage)
Euro	57.6
Japanese yen	13.6
Pound sterling	11.9
Canadian dollar	9.1
Swedish krona	4.2
Swiss franc	3.6

(Source: public information obtained from Intercontinental Exchange, United States)

It can be seen from the above table that the index is heavily weighted towards the euro. Similarly, it is underweighted towards the Canadian dollar (in proportion to US trade with Canada). Many Asian currencies (notably, the Chinese yuan) are absent from the basket. Hence, the index doesn't reflect the actual trade situation of the United States. Despite such a discrepancy, the DXY index is the most popular indicator used to track the US dollar's movements against the leading six currencies.

The value of the DXY index was 100.000 at its start, in March of 1973. The index went on a roller coaster ride after that: it traded as high as 164.720 in February of 1985 and as low as 70.698 in March of 2008 (on a daily closing basis). The rally of the US dollar during the first half of the 1980s led to the Plaza Accord in September of 1985. The agreement between France, West Germany, Japan, the United Kingdom, and the United States depreciated the dollar against the Japanese yen and the Deutsche mark through currency intervention in the forex market. Currency intervention occurs when a central bank buys or sells its currency to raise or lower the value of its currency against another currency. It may be noted that such interventions have only short-term impacts most of the time. Some interventions in the past were carried out secretly; some were made public. In the current media-led environment, any intervention initiated secretly becomes public knowledge quite quickly. Currency speculators make use of such occasions to profit from the volatility in the FX market created by such interventions.

Currency interventions manifest in two forms: sterilised and non-sterilised. In a sterilised intervention, the central bank of a country intervenes in the foreign exchange market without affecting the monetary base. Sterilised intervention is carried out by a central bank when it buys or sells foreign currency bonds with its domestic currency. This action sterilises the effect because it sells or buys an equivalent amount of domestic currency-denominated bonds. Non-sterilised intervention affects the monetary base. In a non-sterilised intervention, the central bank of a country buys or sells foreign currency or foreign currency bonds with domestic currency. In the past few years, there have been several coordinated interventions by leading central banks in the currency market to prevent extreme volatility and bring stability to the exchange rates.

The following table shows the beginning value and the year-end DXY index data for the years 1973–2012:

DXY index from 1973 to 2012 (year-end basis)

As of	Index value	As of	Index value
March 1973	100.000	December 1993	96.840
December 1973	102.390	December 1994	88.720
December 1974	97.290	December 1995	84.760
December 1975	103.510	December 1996	88.120
December 1976	104.560	December 1997	99.650
December 1977	96.440	December 1998	94.170
December 1978	86.500	December 1999	101.870
December 1979	85.820	December 2000	109.560
December 1980	90.390	December 2001	116.750
December 1981	104.690	December 2002	101.850
December 1982	117.360	December 2003	86.920
December 1983	131.790	December 2004	80.850
December 1984	151.470	December 2005	91.170
December 1985	123.460	December 2006	83.650
December 1986	103.590	December 2007	76.695
December 1987	85.400	December 2008	81.308
December 1988	92.530	December 2009	77.860
December 1989	93.160	December 2010	79.028
December 1990	83.120	December 2011	80.178
December 1991	83.530	December 2012	79.769
December 1992	92.360		

The world currency market has been on a roller coaster ride since 1971, when the floating exchange system came into existence. The movements in the US dollar index presented in the previous table provide ample evidence for that assertion.

The DXY index is not a tradable index. Futures and options contracts on the index are traded on the Intercontinental Exchange (ICE).

Chapter 11

Currency Crises since 1971

Introduction

Since the abrogation of the Bretton Woods agreement in 1971, the currency market has gone through several crises. Some crises were not felt immediately; some happened abruptly and caught investors off guard. This section discusses what a currency crisis is and the factors that influence currency crises. In addition, the major crises that occurred since 1971 are reviewed herein.

Currency crisis: definition and meaning

A currency crisis is a situation in which a nation's currency suffers a sudden devaluation that results in speculative attacks on the currency in the foreign exchange market. The crisis negatively affects the country's economy, leading to further exchange rate decline. Thus, a currency crisis is a type of financial crisis, which is often associated with a real economic crisis. A currency crisis is also called a balance-of-payments crisis. At times, a currency crisis can lead to a banking crisis.

Causes of currency crises

There are various reasons behind every currency crisis. However, the presence of *all* those reasons is not necessary for a crisis to develop. A currency crisis can develop due to one or many of the following factors:

- **Deterioration in the economic fundamentals:** A sustained deterioration in the economic fundamentals of a country can adversely affect the country's exchange rate. For example, a rising debt/GDP ratio is a dangerous indicator of a country's deteriorating fundamentals.

- **Rising interest rates:** A sharp rise in interest rates in a country in response to skyrocketing inflation adversely affects the value of that country's currency.

- **Inadequate supervision of the banking and financial sector:** Inadequate supervision of the banking and financial sector will erode investors' confidence in the supervisory authorities of the country. This scenario can lead to massive currency selling.

- **Capital outflows:** Eroding investor confidence in the stability of an economy will result in capital outflows from the country as foreign investors sell their investments and exit the country. Such capital outflows will push the exchange rate lower.

- **War/civil unrest:** Civil unrest of a great magnitude or the outbreak of a war will have negative impacts on the country's currency. The exchange rate will fall sharply in such situations.

- **Rising corruption:** Increase in the corruption level within a country will result in waning investor confidence, which affects the country's exchange rate.

- **External shocks:** External events, even if not directly related to a country, can affect a country's currency due to changing investor perceptions.

- **Market speculation:** Speculative activities in the currency market can either push a country's currency up or down.

Major events/crises in the currency market since 1971

The global currency market has witnessed several shocks, including a few currency crises, since the abrogation of Bretton Woods in 1971. A brief discussion of these events is given here:

- **Nixon shock and the start of Europe's snake in the tunnel (1971–1973):** President Nixon ended US dollar convertibility to gold in 1971. The US dollar was devalued relative to gold. The Smithsonian Agreement was reached in December of 1971. The agreement adjusted the fixed exchange rates established by the Bretton woods conference of 1944 by setting bands of +/—2.25 per cent for currencies to move relative to their central rates against the dollar. This provided a tunnel in which European currencies could trade. The snake in the tunnel was the first attempt at European monetary cooperation, and it was aimed at limiting fluctuations between different European currencies. The tunnel collapsed in 1973 when the US dollar floated freely. As a result, the tunnel became unsustainable.

- **Pegs and floats (1974–1979):** The US dollar continued to fall relative to gold during this period. Most developed countries abandoned their dollar pegs by resorting to a floating regime. Some developing countries chose to maintain their dollar pegs. In March of 1979, the Exchange Rate Mechanism (ERM) was introduced by the European community to reduce exchange rate variability and produce monetary stability in Europe in preparation for the introduction of a single currency.

- **The Plaza Accord (1985):** The sharp appreciation of the US dollar during the 1980–1985 period (and the resultant accumulation of current account deficit by the United States), prompted the G5 nations (France, West Germany, Japan, the United Kingdom, and the United States) to get together in the Plaza Hotel in New York City and sign an agreement known as the Plaza Accord. Signed on 22 September 1985, the agreement was aimed at depreciating the dollar against the other four currencies and reducing the US trade deficit.

- **The Louvre Accord (1987):** The Louvre Accord was signed in Paris on 22 February 1987 by the G6 countries (France, West Germany, Japan, Canada, the United Kingdom, and the United States). The aim was to halt the continued decline in the value of the US dollar caused by the Plaza Accord.

Although the Louvre Accord agreed to put the brakes on the decline of the dollar, the dollar continued to fall after the accord was signed.

- **Black Wednesday (1992):** On Wednesday, 16 September 1992, the United Kingdom decided to exit the ERM and raised its base rate to defend sterling, which came under severe selling pressure.

- **Mexican peso crisis of 1994 (aka the tequila crisis):** During 1994, Mexico suffered a financial crisis as the government's finances deteriorated and the peso fell sharply. The peso was made a free-floating currency by abandoning the fixed band, which resulted in the currency crashing by 80 per cent from 4 to 7.20 pesos per US dollar. Looking at the crisis, it seems that a combination of factors—including the weakening economy, rising inflation, fears of a currency sell off following the assassination of a Mexican presidential candidate, falling foreign reserves, and rising debt—played a part. The significant fall in the peso forced the government to increase domestic interest rates to nearly 80 per cent, which took its toll on the country's GDP. A rescue operation by the United States (through the purchase of pesos and financial assistance to Mexico) brought some relief. The peso started to appreciate starting in 1996.

- **Asian financial crisis of 1997:** The combination of rising national debts and plunging currencies developed into a crisis known as the Asian financial crisis. It affected much of Asia in 1997. The origin of the crisis was in Thailand, and it led to the collapse of the Thai baht, following the government's decision to float the currency and abandon its fixed peg to the US dollar. The sharp rise in the foreign debt-to-GDP ratio in Thailand and other ASEAN nations was the underlying problem. The crisis spread to other Asian countries to varying degrees. It continued to plague the region for much of 1998 and 1999. The crisis started to ease, however, as the decade came to a close.

- **Russian financial crisis of 1998 (aka the ruble crisis):** Russia was hit by a financial crisis, called the Russian financial crisis or ruble crisis during 1998. The chronic fiscal deficit, low natural resource costs, declining productivity, large war debts, artificially high exchange rates, and dependence on foreign capital were the main contributing factors. Russia defaulted on its debt and devalued the ruble on 17 August 1998.

- **Argentine financial crisis from 1999 to 2002:** Argentina went through a financial crisis during the 1999–2002 period. In fact, the crisis started in 1999 with the decrease in real GDP. The crisis led to widespread unemployment, riots, governmental toppling, default on foreign debt, use of alternative currencies, and cessation of the peso's fixed exchange rate to the US dollar. There were signs of optimism by 2002 when the economy started to show some positive trends.

- **Global financial crisis of 2008:** The financial crisis of 2008 was not a currency crisis, per se. However, the disaster took a toll on the foreign exchange market. A number of Asian currencies suffered sharp deteriorations during 2008 and early 2009, with the exception of the yen. For example, the Korean won and Thai baht depreciated by almost 67 per cent and 20 per cent, respectively, against the dollar during a fifteen month period ending in March of 2009. Meanwhile, the yen went up by nearly 22 per cent during 2008. The crisis took its toll on Iceland, too, which witnessed an economic collapse and a plunge of almost 130 per cent in its currency, the Iceland krona. The crisis did not spare the Eurozone. The resultant European debt crisis had its effect on several member countries of the Eurozone, and the euro fell almost 22 per cent against the dollar during the 2008–2010 period. The European debt crisis is yet to see a happy ending; as such, the euro remains volatile.

Chapter 12

Foreign Exchange Reserves

Introduction

Foreign exchange reserves are defined as the foreign currency deposits and bonds held by the central banks and monetary authorities of a country. They are also called forex reserves or FX reserves. Strictly speaking, however, the term should include only foreign currency deposits and bonds. Looked at less strictly, they include a country's gold reserves, special drawing rights (SDRs), and International Monetary Fund (IMF) reserve positions. Hence, in a broad sense, the term *international reserves* is also used.

Further discussion

Because the data on forex reserves are reported to IMF on a confidential basis, the data relating to the composition of forex reserves for individual countries are generally confidential. Still, certain central banks provide reserves data on their websites. The information publicly available from IMF or World Bank is on an aggregate basis. Based on such public data, forex reserves are held mainly in the following seven currencies:

- US dollar
- Euro
- Pound sterling
- Japanese yen
- Canadian dollar
- Australian dollar
- Swiss franc

As per public data available from IMF, the total foreign exchange holdings at the end of 2012 were equivalent to 10.95 trillion USD. Historically, the reserves of advanced economies have far exceeded the reserves of emerging and developing economies. However, the equation has changed drastically over the past decade. As a result, the reserves of developing and emerging countries increased almost five and a half times during the 2003–2012 period. The reserves of advanced economies have increased only two times during the same period. The share of advanced economies has decreased from 58 per cent in 2003 to almost 34 per cent in 2012. Meanwhile, the increase in the share of developing and emerging economies went from 42 per cent to 66 per cent during the same period.

The following table shows the movement in the reserves over the 2003–2012 period for advanced and developing and emerging countries:

Foreign exchange reserves growth (2003–2012)

Description	2003		2012	
	USD (trillions)	Percentage of total	USD (trillions)	Percentage of total
Advanced economies	1.8	58.1	3.7	33.9
Developing and Emerging economies	1.3	41.9	7.2	66.1
Total	**3.1**	**100.0**	**10.9**	**100.0**

A significant part of the current global foreign exchange reserves is held by a small group of countries. It is understood from available data that the top ten holders of foreign exchange reserves account for nearly two-thirds of the world's total foreign currency reserves. China and Japan top the list, accounting for over 40 per cent of the total foreign exchange reserves.

Chapter 13

World Currencies

Introduction

This section provides information on the official world currencies. Most countries have their own form of currency. However, some countries have adopted currencies from other places in the world. In this section, we cover 157 currencies that are used by a total of 217 countries and territories.

Currency categories

Currencies are broadly divided into two categories: hard currency and soft currency.

Hard currency: This form of currency relates to industrialised and politically stable countries. It is accepted as a medium of payment for international transactions. The US dollar, British pound, Euro, Swiss franc, and Japanese yen stand out in the list of hard currencies. The Canadian dollar and Australian dollar are also considered hard currencies. Central banks prefer to keep hard currency in their reserves.

Soft currency: This form of currency is likely to exhibit wild fluctuations. Such currency relates to developing countries with less political and economic stability. Soft currencies are also called weak currencies. Central banks do not prefer to keep soft currencies in their reserves.

Design of currency notes

Designing banknotes is a unique art. Each nation has currency notes of various denominations. Each denomination may feature a different design. Most of the designs reflect a nation's culture and heritage. Some designs depict their founders, famous landmarks, national symbols, or geographical regions. The colour combinations are unique to each nation. However, most banknotes contain security threads, watermarks, and other security systems to deter counterfeiting. Most currencies are printed on a special type of paper to ensure durability. Currency designs undergo periodic changes to deter counterfeiting. Of late, currency designers have become more sensitive to the needs of the visually impaired. Monetary authorities prefer banknotes with sophisticated security features that are inexpensive to produce and very durable. These considerations make the design of banknotes a combination of art, science, and economics. No wonder currency notes are important items for art collectors. Most people don't realise that nearly everyone carries around small pieces of art in his or her wallet.

Design of coins

As in the case of banknote design, designing coins is a unique art. Coins have two sides: obverse and reverse. The obverse of a coin is commonly called its head, and the reverse is often called its tail. The head often depicts an important national figure. Coins of different denominations are produced with different designs on metals, alloys, or synthetic materials. Coins are usually made for subunits of currencies, but several nations have issued coins for the lower denominations of their currencies. When the intrinsic value of the metal used to create the coin exceeds the legal value of the coin, some people collect the coins in large numbers and melt them to extract the metal. The designs of coins are extraordinarily diverse. Coins have also become an important target of art collectors. Coins of interest to collectors include those of historic importance, those with mint errors, and special occasion releases. Coins tossing, the act of throwing a coin in the air to choose between two alternatives, is a popular activity because almost everyone has a coin in his or her wallet.

Information on world currencies

The tables in this chapter provide the key data on different national currencies. These important data include the names of currencies, official codes, subunits, floating statuses, modes of quoting the exchange rates, names of central banks and associated web addresses, denominations of banknotes and coins, and exchange rate at the end of 2012. What follows is a brief description of each of these elements:

- **Currency (currency code):** This field includes the name of the currency, its ISO code, and numeric code.

- **Subunit:** This field includes the various denominations and how they relate to each other.

- **Currency status:** This field indicates whether the currency is fixed (pegged) or floating.

- **Quotation:** This field describes the convention for quoting the currency.

- **Central bank (website):** This field provides the name of the central bank and its associated website.

- **Denomination of banknotes:** This field lists the notes frequently in use. It is possible that some notes listed are not as commonly used as others.

- **Denomination of coins:** This field lists the coins frequently in use. It is possible that some of the coins listed are not as commonly used as others.

- **Exchange rate:** This field shows the exchange rate as at the end of the year 2012.

During the preparation of the data, I made reference to the publicly available data from various sources. These sources include central bank websites, IMF reports, and exchange rate information providers. Though efforts have been made to provide accurate information from such sources, full accuracy is not guaranteed. Readers are urged to check the information or updates provided by relevant central banks from time to time in order to get the most current information on the status of any currency.

Data

The ensuing tables include data about 217 countries and territories. Please note the following special cases:

- 153 countries have their own national currency.

- Seventeen countries in the European Union use the Euro as currency. In addition, five countries outside the EU use the Euro as currency.

- Nine other countries use the Australian dollar as currency.

- Eight other countries use the US dollar as currency.

- Eight countries/territories use the East Caribbean dollar as currency.

- Six countries use the Central African CFA franc as currency.

- Eight countries use the West African CFA franc as currency.

- Zimbabwe has adopted a multi-currency regime.

- French Polynesia, New Caledonia, and Wallis and Futuna use the CFP franc as currency.

- Liechtenstein uses CHF as currency.

The following tables, compiled by the author based on public data mainly from the central bank websites of relative countries, provide the currency data for the countries and territories as discussed previously:

1. AFGHANISTAN

1.	Currency (Currency Code)	:	Afghan afghani (AFN)
	Numeric Code	:	971
2.	Subunit	:	1 AFN = 100 pul
3.	Currency Status	:	Floating
4.	Quotation	:	AFN per US dollar
5.	Central Bank (Website)	:	Da Afghanistan Bank (www.centralbank.gov.af)
6.	Denomination of Banknotes (AFN)	:	1, 2, 5, 10, 20, 50, 100, 500, 1000
7.	Denomination of Coins (AFN)	:	1, 2,5
8.	Exchange Rate (as of Dec. 2012)	:	51.08

2. ALBANIA

1.	Currency (Currency code)	:	Albanian lek (ALL)
	Numeric Code	:	008
2.	Subunit	:	1 ALL = 100 qintars
3.	Currency Status	:	Floating
4.	Quotation	:	ALL per US dollar
5.	Central Bank (Website)	:	Bank of Albania (www.bankofalbania.org)
6.	Denomination of Banknotes (ALL)	:	200, 500, 1000, 2000, 5000
7.	Denomination of Coins (ALL)	:	1,5,10,20,50,100
8.	Exchange Rate (as of Dec.2012)	:	105..88

3. ALGERIA

1.	Currency (Currency code)	:	Algerian dinar (DZD)
	Numeric Code	:	012
2.	Subunit	:	1 DZD = 100 centimes
3.	Currency Status	:	Managed float
4.	Quotation	:	DZD per US dollar
5.	Central Bank (Website)	:	Bank D'Algerie (www.bank-of-algeria.dz)
6.	Denomination of Banknotes (DZD)	:	200, 500, 1000
7.	Denomination of Coins (DZD)	:	5, 10, 20, 50
8.	Exchange Rate (as of Dec.2012)	:	78.85

4. ANGOLA

1.	Currency (Currency Code)	:	Angolan kwanza (AOA)
	Numeric Code	:	973
2.	Subunit	:	1 AOA = 100 centimos
3.	Currency Status	:	Managed float
4.	Quotation	:	AOA per US dollar
5.	Central Bank (Website)	:	Banco Nacional de Angola (www.bna.ao)
6.	Denomination of Banknotes (AOA)	:	10, 50, 100, 200, 500, 1000, 2000
7.	Denomination of Coins (AOA)	:	1,2,5
8.	Exchange Rate (as of Dec.2012)	:	95.82

5. ARGENTINA

1.	Currency (Currency Code)	:	Argentine peso (ARS)
	Numeric Code	:	032
2.	Subunit	:	1 ARS = 100 centavos
3.	Currency Status	:	Floating
4.	Quotation	:	ARS per US dollar
5.	Central Bank (Website)	:	Central Bank of Argentina (www.bcra.gov.ar)
6.	Denomination of Banknotes (ARS)	:	2,5,10,20,50,100
7.	Denomination of Coins (ARS/ Centavos)	:	ARS: 1,2 Centavos: 1,5,10,25,50
8.	Exchange Rate (as of Dec. 2012)	:	4.91

6. ARMENIA

1.	Currency (Currency Code)	:	Armenian dram (AMD)
	Numeric Code	:	051
2.	Subunit	:	1 AMD = 100 louma
3.	Currency Status	:	Floating
4.	Quotation	:	AMD per US dollar
5.	Central Bank (Website)	:	Central Bank of Armenia (www.cba.am)
6.	Denomination of Banknotes (AMD)	:	500,1000,5000,10000,20000,50 000,100000
7.	Denomination of Coins (AMD)	:	10,20,50,100,200,500
8.	Exchange Rate (as of Dec. 2012)	:	403.58

7. ARUBA

1.	Currency (Currency Code)	:	Aruban guilder (aka Aruban
	Numeric Code	:	florin) (AWG)
			533
2.	Subunit	:	1 AWG = 100 cents
3.	Currency Status	:	Pegged to the US dollar
4.	Quotation	:	AWG per US dollar
5.	Central Bank (Website)	:	Central Bank Van Aruba
			(www.cbaruba.org)
6.	Denomination of Banknotes (AWG)	:	10,25,50,100,500
7.	Denomination of Coins (AWG/ Cents	:	Florin: 1,5
			Cents: 5,10,25,50
8.	Exchange Rate (as of Dec. 2012)	:	1.78

8. AUSTRALIA

1.	Currency (Currency Code)	:	Australian dollar (AUD)
	Numeric Code	:	036
2.	Subunit	:	1 AUD = 100 cents
3.	Currency Status	:	Free-floating
4.	Quotation	:	US dollar per AUD
5.	Central Bank (Website)	:	Reserve Bank of Australia
			(www.rba.gov.au)
6.	Denomination of Banknotes (AUD)	:	5,10,20,50,100
7.	Denomination of Coins (AUD/ Cents)	:	AUD: 1,2
			Cents: 5,10,20,50
8.	Exchange Rate History (USD per 1 AUD, as of Dec. 2012))	:	1.03

9.	Countries Using AUD as Currency	:	Ashmore and Cartier Islands, Christmas Island, Cocos Islands, Coral Sea Islands, Kiribati, Nauru, Norfolk Island, Territory of Papua and New Guinea, and Tuvalu.

9. AZERBAIJAN

1.	Currency (Currency Code) Numeric Code	: :	Azerbaijani manat (AZN) 944
2.	Subunit	:	1 AZN = 100 qepik
3.	Currency Status	:	Floating
4.	Quotation	:	AZN per US dollar
5.	Central Bank (Website)	:	Central Bank of the Republic of Azerbaijan (www.cbar.az)
6.	Denomination of Banknotes (AZN)	:	1, 2, 5, 10, 20, 50, 100
7.	Denomination of Coins (AZN)	:	1, 3, 5, 10, 20, 50
8.	Exchange Rate (as of Dec. 2012)	:	0.75

10. BAHAMAS

1.	Currency (Currency Code) Numeric Code	: :	Bahamian dollar (BSD) 044
2.	Subunit	:	1 BSD = 100 cents
3.	Currency Status	:	Pegged to the US dollar (1:1)
4.	Quotation	:	BSD per US dollar
5.	Central Bank (Website)	:	The Central Bank of the Bahamas (www.centralbankbahamas.com)

6.	Denomination of Banknotes (BSD)	:	1,5,10,20,50,100
7.	Denomination of Coins (BSD)	:	1,5,10,25
8.	Exchange Rate (as of Dec. 2012)	:	1.00

11. BAHRAIN

1.	Currency (Currency Code)	:	Bahraini dinar (BHD)
	Numeric Code	:	048
2.	Subunit	:	1 BHD = 1000 fils
3.	Currency Status	:	Pegged to the US dollar (0.38:1)
4.	Quotation	:	BHD per US dollar
5.	Central Bank (Website)	:	Central Bank of Bahrain (www.cbb.gov.bh)
6.	Denomination of Banknotes (BHD)	:	½,1,5,10,20
7.	Denomination of Coins (Fils)	:	5,10,25,50,100,500
8.	Exchange Rate (as of Dec. 2012)	:	0.377

12. BANGLADESH

1.	Currency (Currency Code)	:	Bangladesh taka (BDT)
	Numeric Code	:	050
2.	Subunit	:	1 BDT = 100 poisha
3.	Currency Status	:	Managed float
4.	Quotation	:	BDT per US dollar
5.	Central Bank (Website)	:	Bangladesh Bank (www.bangladeshbank.org.bd)
6.	Denomination of Banknotes (BDT)	:	2,5,10,25

7.	Denomination of Coins (BDT/ Poisha)	:	BDT: 1,2,5 Poisha: 1,5,10,25,50
8.	Exchange Rate (as of Dec.2012)	:	79.78

13. BARBADOS

1.	Currency (Currency Code)	:	Barbadian dollar (BBD)
	Numeric Code	:	052
2.	Subunit	:	1 BBD = 100 cents
3.	Currency Status	:	Pegged to the US dollar
4.	Quotation	:	BBD per US dollar
5.	Central Bank (Website)	:	Central Bank of Barbados (www.centralbank.org.bb)
6.	Denomination of Banknotes (BBD)	:	2,5,10,20,50,100
7.	Denomination of Coins (BBD/ Cents)	:	BBD: 1 Cents: 1,5,10,25
8.	Exchange Rate (as of Dec.2012)	:	2.00

14. BELARUS

1.	Currency (Currency Code)	:	Belarusian ruble (BYR)
	Numeric Code	:	974
2.	Subunit	:	1 BYR = 100 kopeks
3.	Currency Status	:	Managed float
4.	Quotation	:	BYR per US dollar
5.	Central Bank (Website)	:	National Bank of the Republic of Belarus (www.nbrb.by)

6.	Denomination of Banknotes (BYR)	:	100,500,1000,5000,10000,2000 0,50000, 100000
7.	Denomination of Coins	:	Not used
8.	Exchange Rate (as of Dec.2012)	:	8552.50

15. BELIZE

1.	Currency (Currency Code)	:	Belizean dollar (BZD)
	Numeric Code	:	084
2.	Subunit	:	1 BZD = 100 cents
3.	Currency Status	:	Pegged to the US dollar (2:1)
4.	Quotation	:	BZD per US dollar
5.	Central Bank (Website)	:	Central Bank of Belize (www.centralbank.org.bz)
6.	Denomination of Banknotes (BZD)	:	2,5,10,20,50,100
7.	Denomination of Coins (BZD/ Cents)	:	BZD: 1,2 Cents: 1,5,10,25,50
8.	Exchange Rate (as of Dec.2012)	:	1.99

16. BERMUDA

1.	Currency (Currency Code)	:	Bermudian dollar (BMD)
	Numeric Code	:	060
2.	Subunit	:	1 BMD = 100 cents
3.	Currency Status	:	Pegged to the US dollar (1:1)
4.	Quotation	:	BMD per US dollar
5.	Central Bank (Website)	:	Bermuda Monetary Authority (www.bma.bm)

6.	Denomination of Banknotes (BMD)	:	2,5,10,20,50,100
7.	Denomination of Coins (BMD/Cents)	:	BMD: 1 Cents: 1,5,10,25,50
8.	Exchange Rate (as of Dec. 2012)	:	1.00

17. BHUTAN

1.	Currency (Currency Code) Numeric Code	: :	Bhutanese ngultrum (BTN) 064
2.	Subunit	:	1 BTN = 100 chhertum
3.	Currency Status	:	Linked at parity to the Indian rupee
4.	Quotation	:	BTN per US dollar
5.	Central Bank (Website)	:	Royal Monetary Authority of Bhutan (www.rma.org.bt)
6.	Denomination of Banknotes (BTN)	:	1,5,10,20,50,100,500,1000
7.	Denomination of Coins (BTN/ Chhertum)	:	BTN: 1 Chhertum: 20,25,50
8.	Exchange Rate (as of Dec. 2012)	:	54.77

18. BOLIVIA

1.	Currency (Currency Code) Numeric Code	: :	Bolivian boliviano (BOB) 068
2.	Subunit	:	1 BOB = 100 centavos
3.	Currency Status	:	Managed float
4.	Quotation	:	BOB per US dollar
5.	Central Bank (Website)	:	Banco Central de Bolivia (www.bcb.gob.bo)

6.	Denomination of Banknotes (BOB)	:	200,100,50,20,10
7.	Denomination of Coins (BOB/ Centavos)	:	BOB: 5,2,1 Centavos: 50,20,10
8.	Exchange Rate (as of Dec.2012)	:	6.97

19. BOSNIA and HERZEGOVINA

1.	Currency (Currency Code) Numeric Code	: :	Bosnia and Herzegovinian marka (BAM) 977
2.	Subunit	:	1 BAM = 100 pfenniga (fening)
3.	Currency Status	:	Pegged to the euro (1:0.51)
4.	Quotation	:	BAM per US dollar
5.	Central Bank (Website)	:	Central Bank of Bosnia and Herzegovina (www.cbbh.ba)
6.	Denomination of Banknotes (BAM)	:	10,20,50,100,200
7.	Denomination of Coins (BAM/Pfenniga)	:	BAM: 1,2,5 Pfenniga: 5,10,20,50
8.	Exchange Rate (as of Dec.2012)	:	1.48

20. BOTSWANA

1.	Currency (Currency Code) Numeric Code	: :	Botswana pula (BWP) 072
2.	Subunit	:	1 BWP = 100 thebe
3.	Currency Status	:	Pegged to a basket of currencies
4.	Quotation	:	BWP per US dollar
5.	Central Bank (Website)	:	Bank of Botswana (www.bankofbotswana.bw)

6.	Denomination of Banknotes (BWP)	:	10,20,50,100,200
7.	Denomination of Coins (BWP/Theba)	:	BWP: 1,2,5 Theba: 5,10,25,50
8.	Exchange Rate (as of Dec. 2012)	:	7.81

21. BRAZIL

1.	Currency (Currency Code) Numeric Code	: :	Brazilian real (BRL) 986
2.	Subunit	:	1 BRL = 100 centavos
3.	Currency Status	:	Floating
4.	Quotation	:	BRL per US dollar
5.	Central Bank (Website)	:	Central Bank of Brazil (www.bcb.gov.br)
6.	Denomination of Banknotes (BRL)	:	5,10,20,50,100
7.	Denomination of Coins (BRL/Centavo)	:	BRL: 1 Centavos: 5,10,25,50
8.	Exchange Rate (as of Dec.2012)	:	2.05

22. BRUNEI DARUSSALAM

1.	Currency (Currency Code) Numeric Code	: :	Brunei dollar (BND) 096
2.	Subunit	:	1 BND = 100 cents
3.	Currency Status	:	Pegged to the Singapore dollar
4.	Quotation	:	BND per US dollar
5.	Central Bank (Website)	:	Autoribi Monetari Brunei Darussalam (www.ambd. gov.bn)

6.	Denomination of Banknotes (BND)	:	1,5,10
7.	Denomination of Coins (Cents)	:	1,5,10,20,50
8.	Exchange Rate (as of Dec. 2012)	:	1.21

23. BULGARIA

1.	Currency (Currency Code)	:	Bulgarian lev (BGN)
	Numeric Code	:	975
2.	Subunit	:	1 BGN = 100 stotinki
3.	Currency Status	:	Pegged to the euro
4.	Quotation	:	BGN per US dollar
5.	Central Bank (Website)	:	Bulgarian National Bank (www.bnb.bg)
6.	Denomination of Banknotes (BGN)	:	1,2,5,10,20,50,100
7.	Denomination of Coins (BGN/Stotinki)	:	BGN: 1 Stotinki: 1,2,5,10,20,50
8.	Exchange Rate (as of Dec. 2012)	:	1.48

24. BURUNDI

1.	Currency (Currency Code)	:	Burundian franc (BIF)
	Numeric Code	:	108
2.	Subunit	:	1 BIF = 100 centimes
3.	Currency Status	:	Pegged to a basket of currencies
4.	Quotation	:	BIF per US dollar
5.	Central Bank (Website)	:	The Bank of the Republic of Burundi (www.brb.bi)
6.	Denomination of Banknotes (BIF)	:	10, 20, 0, 100, 500, 1000, 2000, 5000, 10000

7.	Denomination of Coins (BIF)	:	1,5
8.	Exchange Rate (as of Dec.2012)	:	1542.00

25. CAMBODIA

1.	Currency (Currency Code)	:	Cambodian riel (KHR)
	Numeric Code	:	116
2.	Subunit	:	1 KHR = 100 sen
3.	Currency Status	:	Managed float
4.	Quotation	:	KHR per US dollar
5.	Central Bank (Website)	:	National Bank of Cambodia (www.nbc.org.kh)
6.	Denomination of Banknotes (KHR)	:	100,500,1000,2000,5000,10000,20000,50000
7.	Denomination of Coins (KHR)	:	KHR: 500,200,100,50
8.	Exchange Rate (as of Dec.2012)	:	4000.00

26. CANADA

1.	Currency (Currency Code)	:	Canadian dollar (CAD)
	Numeric Code	:	124
2.	Subunit	:	1 CAD = 100 cents
3.	Currency Status	:	Free-floating
4.	Quotation	:	USD per CAD
5.	Central Bank (Website)	:	Bank of Canada (www.bankofcanada.ca)
6.	Denomination of Banknotes (CAD)	:	5,10,20,50,100
7.	Denomination of Coins (CAD/Cents)	:	CAD: 1,2 Cents: 1,5,10,25,50

8.	Exchange Rate (USD per CAD, as of Dec.2012)	:	1.01

27. CAPE VERDE

1.	Currency (Currency Code)	:	Cape Verdean escudo (CVE)
	Numeric Code	:	132
2.	Subunit	:	1 CVE = 100 centavos
3.	Currency Status	:	Pegged to the euro (10.27:1)
4.	Quotation	:	CVE per EUR
5.	Central Bank (Website)	:	Bank of Cape Verde (www.bcv.cv)
6.	Denomination of Banknotes (CVE)	:	200,500,1000,2000,2500,5000
7.	Denomination of Coins (CVE)	:	1,5,10,20,50,100
8.	Exchange Rate (CVE per EUR, as of Dec. 2012)	:	111.64

28. CAYMAN ISLANDS

1.	Currency (Currency Code)	:	Cayman Islands dollar (KYD)
	Numeric Code	:	136
2.	Subunit	:	1 KYD = 100 cents
3.	Currency Status	:	Pegged to the US dollar (1.22:1)
4.	Quotation	:	US dollar per KYD
5.	Central Bank (Website)	:	Cayman Islands Monetary Authority (www.cimoney.com.ky)

6.	Denomination of Banknotes (KYD)	:	1,5,10,25,50,100
7.	Denomination of Coins (Cents)	:	1,5,10,25
8.	Exchange Rate (USD per KYD, as of Dec. 2012)	:	1.22

29. CENTRAL AFRICAN REPUBLIC

1.	Currency (Currency Code)	:	CFA franc (XAF)
	Numeric Code	:	950
2.	Subunit	:	1 CFA = 100 centimes
3.	Currency Status	:	Pegged to the euro (655.95:1)
4.	Quotation	:	XAF per US dollar
5.	Central Bank (Website)	:	Bank of Central African States (www.beac.int)
6.	Denomination of Banknotes (XAF)	:	500,1000,2000,5000,10000
7.	Denomination of Coins (XAF)	:	1,2,5,10,25,50,100,500
8.	Exchange Rate (as of Dec. 2012)	:	496.38
9.	Countries Using XAF	:	Cameroon, The Central African Republic, Chad, Congo, Equatorial Guinea, and Gabon.

30. CHILE

1.	Currency (Currency Code)	:	Chilean peso (CLP)
	Numeric Code	:	152
2.	Subunit	:	1 CLP = 100 centavos
3.	Currency Status	:	Free-floating
4.	Quotation	:	CLP per US dollar

5.	Central Bank (Website)	:	Banco Central de Chile (www.bcentral.cl)
6.	Denomination of Banknotes (CLP)	:	1000, 2000, 5000, 10000, 20000
7.	Denomination of Coins (CLP)	:	1,5,50,100,500
8.	Exchange Rate (as of Dec. 2012)	:	479.05

31. CHINA

1.	Currency (Currency Code) Numeric Code	: :	Chinese renminbi (aka Yuan) (CNY) 156
2.	Subunit	:	1 CNY = 100 fen, 1 CNY = 10 jiao, 1 jiao = 10 fen
3.	Currency Status	:	Pegged to a basket of currencies and managed non-deliverables
4.	Quotation	:	CNY per US dollar
5.	Central Bank (Website)	:	People's Bank of China (www.pbc.gov.cn)
6.	Denomination of Banknotes (CNY)	:	1,2,5,10,20,50,100
7.	Denomination of Coins (FEN)	:	1,2,5
8.	Exchange Rate (as of Dec. 2012)	:	6.23

32. COLOMBIA

1.	Currency (Currency Code) Numeric Code	: :	Colombian peso (COP) 170
2.	Subunit	:	1 COP = 100 centavos
3.	Currency Status	:	Floating with managed currency regime
4.	Quotation	:	COP per US dollar

5.	Central Bank (Website)	:	Banco de la Republica (www.banrep.gov.co)
6.	Denomination of Banknotes (COP)	:	1000, 2000, 5000, 10000, 20000, 50000
7.	Denomination of Coins (COP)	:	50,100,200,500
8.	Exchange Rate(as of Dec. 2012)	:	1767.50

33. COMOROS

1.	Currency (Currency Code)	:	Comorian franc (KMF)
	Numeric Code	:	174
2.	Subunit	:	1 KMF = 100 centimes
3.	Currency Status	:	Pegged to the euro (491.97:1)
4.	Quotation	:	KMF per US dollar
5.	Central Bank (Website)	:	Central Bank of the Comoros (www.banque-comores.km)
6.	Denomination of Banknotes (KMF)	:	500,1000,2000,5000,10000
7.	Denomination of Coins (KMF)	:	25,50,100
8.	Exchange Rate (as of Dec. 2012)	:	373.07

34. DEMOCRATIC REPUBLIC OF CONGO (KINSHASA)

1.	Currency (Currency Code)	:	Congolese franc (CDF)
	Numeric Code	:	976
2.	Subunit	:	1 CDF = 100 centimes
3.	Currency Status	:	Managed
4.	Quotation	:	CDF per US dollar
5.	Central Bank (Website)	:	Bank Centrale du Congo (www.bcc.cd)

6.	Denomination of Banknotes (CDF)	:	CDF: 5, 10, 20, 50, 100, 200, 500, 1000, 5000, 10000, 20000 Centimes: 1,5,10,20,50
7.	Denomination of Coins (CDF)	:	None used
8.	Exchange Rate (as of Dec. 2012)	:	915.00

35. COSTA RICA

1.	Currency (Currency Code)	:	Costa Rican colon (CRC)
	Numeric Code	:	188
2.	Subunit	:	1 CRC = 100 centimes
3.	Currency Status	:	Managed float
4.	Quotation	:	CRC per US dollar
5.	Central Bank (Website)	:	Central Bank of Costa Rica (www.bccr.fi.cr)
6.	Denomination of Banknotes (CRC)	:	1000,2000, 5000, 10000, 20000, 50000
7.	Denomination of Coins (CRC)	:	1,5,10,20,50,100,500
8.	Exchange Rate (as of Dec. 2012)	:	510.70

36. CROATIA

1.	Currency (Currency Code)	:	Croatian kuna (HRK)
	Numeric Code	:	191
2.	Subunit	:	1 HRK = 100 lipa
3.	Currency Status	:	Managed float
4.	Quotation	:	HRK per US dollar
5.	Central Bank (Website)	:	Crotian National Bank (www.hnb.hr)

6.	Denomination of Banknotes (HRK)	:	10,20,50,100,200
7.	Denomination of Coins (HRK)	:	HRK: 1,2,5 Lipa: 5,10,20,50
8.	Exchange Rate (as of Dec. 2012)	:	5.71

37. CUBA

1.	Currency (Currency Code) Numeric Code	: :	Cuban peso (CUP)/convertible peso (CUC) 192/931
2.	Subunit	:	1 CUP = 100 centavos
3.	Currency Status	:	CUP: non-convertible fixed rate linked to the US dollar CUC: convertible peso
4.	Quotation	:	CUP per US dollar
5.	Central Bank (Website)	:	Central Bank of Cuba (www.bc.gov.cu)
7.	Denomination of Banknotes (CUC)	:	1,3,5,10,20,50,100
8.	Denomination of Coins (CUC)	:	CUC: 1,3 Centavos: 1,5,20
9.	Exchange Rate (as of Dec.2012)	:	1.00

38. CZECH REPUBLIC

1.	Currency (Currency Code) Numeric Code	: :	Czech koruna (CZK) 203
2.	Subunit	:	1 CZK = 100 halero
3.	Currency Status	:	Free-floating
4.	Quotation	:	CZK per US dollar

5.	Central Bank (Website)	:	Czech National Bank (www.cnb.cz)
6.	Denomination of Banknotes (CZK)	:	100,200,500,1000
7.	Denomination of Coins (CZK)	:	1,2,5,10,20,50
8.	Exchange Rate (as of Dec. 2012)	:	19.00

39. DENMARK

1.	Currency (Currency Code)	:	Danish krone (DKK)
	Numeric Code	:	208
2.	Subunit	:	1 DKK = 100 ore
3.	Currency Status	:	Linked to the euro (7.46 DKK, +/—2.25%)
4.	Quotation	:	DKK per US dollar
5.	Central Bank (Website)	:	Denmark National Bank (www.nationalbanken.dk)
6.	Denomination of Banknotes (DKK)	:	50,100,200,500,1000
7.	Denomination of Coins (DKK/ ORE)	:	DKK: 1,2,5,10,20 ORE: 50
8	Exchange Rate (as of Dec. 2012)	:	5.65

40. DJIBOUTI

1.	Currency (Currency Code)	:	Djiboutian franc (DJF)
	Numeric Code	:	262
2.	Subunit	:	1 DJF = 100 centimes
3.	Currency Status	:	Pegged to US dollar (177.72:1)
4.	Quotation	:	DJF per US dollar

5.	Central Bank (Website)	:	Central Bank of Djibouti (www.banque-centrale.dj)
6.	Denomination of Banknotes (DJF)	:	1000,2000,5000,10000
7.	Denomination of Coins (DJF)	:	DJF: 1,2,5,10,20,50,100,500
8.	Exchange Rate (as of Dec. 2012)	:	180.50

41. DOMINICAN REPUBLIC

1.	Currency (Currency Code) Numeric Code	: :	Dominican Republic peso (DOP) 951
2.	Subunit	:	1 DOP = 100 centavos
3.	Currency Status	:	Managed float
4.	Quotation	:	DOP per US dollar
5.	Central Bank (Website)	:	Central Bank of Dominican Republic (www.bancentral.gov.do)
6.	Denomination of Banknotes (DOP)	:	20, 50, 100, 200,500, 1000, 2000
7.	Denomination of Coins (DOP)	:	1,5,10,25
8.	Exchange Rate (as of Dec. 2012)	:	40.15

42. EAST CARIBBEAN STATES

1.	Currency (Currency Code) Numeric Code	: :	East Caribbean dollar (XCD)
2.	Subunit	:	1 XCD = 100 cents
3.	Currency Status	:	Pegged to the US dollar (2.70:1)
4.	Quotation	:	XCD per US dollar
5.	Central Bank (Website)	:	East Caribbean Central Bank (www.eccb-centralbank.org)

6.	Denomination of Banknotes (XCD)	:	5,10,20,50,100
7.	Denomination of Coins (XCD/ Cents)	:	XCD: 1,2 Cents: 1,2,5,10,25
8.	Countries Using XCD as Currency	:	Anguilla, Antigua and Barbuda, Dominica, Granada, Montserrat, Saint Kitts and Nevis, Saint Lucia, and Saint Vincent and the Grenadines.

43. EGYPT

1.	Currency (Currency Code) Numeric Code	: :	Egyptian pound (EGP) 818
2.	Subunit	:	1 EGP = 100 piastres
3.	Currency Status	:	Floating
4.	Quotation	:	EGP per US dollar
5.	Central Bank (Website)	:	Central Bank of Egypt (www.cbe.org.eg)
6.	Day Count Convention	:	Actual/360
7.	Denomination of Banknotes (EGP)	:	EGP: 5,10,20,50,100,200
8.	Denomination of Coins (EGP/ Piastres)	:	EGP: 1 Piastres: 25,50
9.	Exchange Rate (as of Dec. 2012)	:	6.19

44. ERITREA

| 1. | Currency (Currency Code)
Numeric Code | :
: | Eritrean nakfa (ERN)
232 |
| 2. | Subunit | : | 1 ERN = 100 cents |

3.	Currency Status	:	Managed float
4.	Quotation	:	ERN per US dollar
5.	Central Bank (Website)	:	Bank of Eritrea (www.boe.gov.er)
6.	Denomination of Banknotes (ERN)	:	ERN: 1,5,10,20,50,100
7.	Denomination of Coins (ERN/ Cents)	:	ERN: 1 Cents: 1,5,10,25,50
8.	Exchange Rate (as of Dec. 2012)	:	15.10

45. ETHIOPIA

1.	Currency (Currency Code) Numeric Code	: :	Ethiopian birr (ETB) 230
2.	Subunit	:	1 ETB = 100 cents
3.	Currency Status	:	Managed float
4.	Quotation	:	ETB per US dollar
5.	Central Bank (Website)	:	National Bank of Ethiopia (www.nbe.gov.et)
6.	Denomination of Banknotes (ETB)	:	1,5,10,50,100
7.	Denomination of Coins (ETB/ Cents)	:	ETB: 1 Cents: 1,5,10,25,50
8.	Exchange Rate (as of Dec. 2012)	:	18.22

46. FALKLAND ISLANDS

1.	Currency (Currency Code) Numeric Code	: :	Falkland Islands pound (FKP) 238
2.	Subunit	:	1 FKP = 100 pence
3.	Currency Status	:	Linked at parity with the GBP

4.	Quotation	:	US dollar per FKP
5.	Central Bank (Website)	:	Government of the Falkland Islands (www.falklands.gov.fk)
6.	Denomination of Banknotes (FKP)	:	5,10,20,50
7.	Denomination of Coins (FKP/ Pence)	:	FKP: 1,2 Pence: 1,2,5,10,20,50
8.	Exchange Rate (as of Dec. 2012)	:	1.61

47. FIJI

1.	Currency (Currency Code) Numeric Code	: :	Fijian dollar (FJD) 242
2.	Subunit	:	1 FJD = 100 cents
3.	Currency Status	:	Pegged to a basket of currencies
4.	Quotation	:	US dollar per FJD
5.	Central Bank (Website)	:	Reserve Bank of Fiji (www.reservebank.gov.fj)
6.	Denomination of Banknotes (FJD)	:	2,5,10,20,50,100
7.	Denomination of Coins (FJD/ Cents)	:	FJD: 1 Cents: 5,10,20,50
8.	Exchange Rate (USD per FJD, as of Dec. 2012)	:	0.55

48. FRENCH POLYNESIA

| 1. | Currency (Currency Code) Numeric Code | : : | CFP franc (XPF) 953 |
| 2. | Subunit | : | 1 XPF = 100 centimes |

3.	Currency Status	:	Pegged to the euro (1:0.01)
4.	Quotation	:	XPF per US dollar
5.	Central Bank (Website)	:	L'Institut d'Emission d'Outre—Mer (www.ieom.fr)
6.	Denomination of Banknotes (XPF)	:	500,1000,5000,10000
7.	Denomination of Coins (XPF)	:	1,2,5,20,50,100
8.	Exchange Rate (as of Dec. 2012)	:	90.30
9.	Countries Using XPF as Currency	:	New Caledonia and Wallis and Futuna

49. GAMBIA

1.	Currency (Currency Code)	:	Gambian dalasi (GMD)
	Numeric Code	:	270
2.	Subunit	:	1 GMD = 100 butut
3.	Currency Status	:	Floating
4.	Quotation	:	GMD per US dollar
5.	Central Bank (Website)	:	Central Bank of the Gambia (www.cbg.gm)
6.	Day Count Convention	:	Actual/360
7.	Denomination of Banknotes (GMD)	:	100,50,25,10,5
8.	Denomination of Coins (GMD/Butut)	:	GMD: 1 Butut: 1,5,10,25,50
9.	Exchange Rate (as of Dec. 2012)	:	35.00

50. GEORGIA

1.	Currency (Currency Code)	:	Georgian lari (GEL)
	Numeric Code	:	981
2.	Subunit	:	1 GEL = 100 tetri
3.	Currency Status	:	Managed float
4.	Quotation	:	GEL per US dollar
5.	Central Bank (Website)	:	National Bank of Georgia (www.nbg.gov.ge)
6.	Denomination of Banknotes (GEL)	:	5,10,20,50
7.	Denomination of Coins (GEL/Tetri)	:	GEL: 1,2 Tetri: 1,2,5,10,20,50
8.	Exchange Rate (as of Dec. 2012)	:	1.65

51. GHANA

1.	Currency (Currency Code)	:	New Ghana cedi (GHS)
	Numeric Code	:	936
2.	Subunit	:	1 GHS = 100 pesewas
3.	Currency Status	:	Floating
4.	Quotation	:	GHS per US dollar
5.	Central Bank (Website)	:	Bank of Ghana (www.bog.gov.gh)
6.	Denomination of Banknotes (GHS)	:	1,2,5,10,20,50
7.	Denomination of Coins (GHS/Pesewas)	:	GHS: 1 Pesewas: 1,5,10,20,50
8.	Exchange Rate (as of Dec. 2012)	:	1.90

52. GIBRALTAR

1.	Currency (Currency Code)	:	Gibraltar pound (GIP)
	Numeric Code	:	292
2.	Subunit	:	1 GIP = 100 pence
3.	Currency Status	:	Linked to the GBP at parity
4.	Quotation	:	US dollar per GIP
5.	Central Bank (Website)	:	Government of Gibraltar (www.gibraltar.gov.gi)
6.	Denomination of Banknotes (GIP)	:	5,10,20,50,100
7.	Denomination of Coins (GIP/ Pence)	:	GIP: 1,2,5 Pence: 1,2,5,10,20,50
8.	Exchange Rate (USD per GIP, as of Dec. 2012)	:	1.61

53. GUATEMALA

1.	Currency (Currency Code)	:	Guatemalan quetzal (GTQ)
	Numeric Code	:	320
2.	Subunit	:	1 GTQ = 100 centavos
3.	Currency Status	:	Floating
4.	Quotation	:	GTQ per US dollar
5.	Central Bank (Website)	:	Bank of Guatemala (www.banguat.gob.gt)
6.	Denomination of Banknotes (GTQ)	:	5,10,20,50,100
7.	Denomination of Coins (GTQ/Centavos)	:	GTQ: 1 Centavos: 1,5,10,25,50
8.	Exchange Rate (as of Dec. 2012)	:	7.90

54. GUINEA

1.	Currency (Currency Code)	:	Guinean franc (GNF)
	Numeric Code	:	324
2.	Subunit	:	1 GNF = 100 centime
3.	Currency Status	:	Managed
4.	Quotation	:	GNF per US dollar
5.	Central Bank (Website)	:	Central Bank of the Republic of Guinea (www.bcrg-guinee.org)
6.	Denomination of Banknotes (GNF)	:	100,500,1000,5000,10000
7.	Denomination of Coins (GNF)	:	1,5,10,25,50
8.	Exchange Rate (as of Dec. 2012)	:	7008.00

55. GUYANA

1.	Currency (Currency Code)	:	Guyanese dollar (GYD)
	Numeric Code	:	328
2.	Subunit	:	1 GY D= 100 cents
3.	Currency Status	:	Floating
4.	Quotation	:	GYD per US dollar
5.	Central Bank (Website)	:	Bank of Guyana (www.bankofguyana,org.gy)
6.	Denomination of Banknotes (GYD)	:	20,100,500,1000
7.	Denomination of Coins (GYD)	:	1,5,10
8.	Exchange Rate (as of Dec. 2012)	:	203.95

56. HAITI

1.	Currency (Currency Code)	:	Haitian gourde (HTG)
	Numeric Code	:	332
2.	Subunit	:	1 HTG = 100 centimes
3.	Currency Status	:	Free-floating
4.	Quotation	:	HTG per US dollar
5.	Central Bank (Website)	:	Bank of the Republic of Haiti (www.brh.net)
6.	Denomination of Banknotes (HTG)	:	10,25,50,100,250,500,1000
7.	Denomination of Coins (HTG/Centimes)	:	HTG: 1,5 Centimes: 5,10,20,50
8.	Exchange Rate (as of Dec. 2012)	:	42.65

57. HONDURAS

1.	Currency (Currency Code)	:	Honduran lempira (HNL)
	Numeric Code	:	340
2.	Subunit	:	1 HNL = 100 centavos
3.	Currency Status	:	Managed float
4.	Quotation	:	HNL per US dollar
5.	Central Bank (Website)	:	Banco Central de Honduras (www.bch.hn)
6.	Denomination of Banknotes (HNL)	:	1,2,5,10,20,50,100,500
7.	Denomination of Coins (HNL)	:	10,20,50
8.	Exchange Rate (as of Dec. 2012)	:	19.86

58. HONG KONG

1.	Currency (Currency Code)	:	Hong Kong dollar (HKD)
	Numeric Code	:	344
2.	Subunit	:	1 HKD = 100 cents
3.	Currency Status	:	Linked to USD (7.8:1)
4.	Quotation	:	HKD per US dollar
5.	Central Bank (Website)	:	Hong Kong Monetary Authority (www.info.gov.hk/hkma)
6.	Denomination of Banknotes (HKD)	:	10,20,50,100,150,500,1000
7.	Denomination of Coins (HKD/Cents)	:	HKD: 1,2,5,10 Cents: 10,20,50
8.	Exchange Rate (as of Dec. 2012)	:	7.75

59. HUNGARY

1.	Currency (Currency Code)	:	Hungarian forint (HUF)
	Numeric Code	:	348
2.	Subunit	:	1 HUF = 100 filler
3.	Currency Status	:	Floating
4.	Quotation	:	HUF per US dollar
5.	Central Bank (Website)	:	Hungarian National Bank (www.mnb.hu)
6.	Denomination of Banknotes (HUF)	:	500, 1000, 2000, 5000, 10000, 20000
7.	Denomination of Coins (HUF)	:	5,10,20,50,100,200
8.	Exchange Rate (as of Dec. 2012)	:	220.47

60. ICELAND

1.	Currency (Currency Code)	:	Icelandic krona (ISK)
	Numeric Code	:	352
2.	Subunit	:	1 ISK = 100 aurar
3.	Currency Status	:	Managed float
4.	Quotation	:	ISK per US dollar
5.	Central Bank (Website)	:	Central Bank of Iceland (www.sedlabanki.is)
6.	Denomination of Banknotes (ISK)	:	500,1000,2000,5000
7.	Denomination of Coins (ISK)	:	1,5,10,50,100
8.	Exchange Rate (as of Dec. 2012)	:	128.64

61. INDIA

1.	Currency (Currency Code)	:	Indian rupee (INR)
	Numeric Code	:	356
2.	Subunit	:	1 INR = 100 paise
3.	Currency Status	:	Managed float
4.	Quotation	:	INR per US dollar
5.	Central Bank (Website)	:	Reserve Bank of India (www.rbi.org.in)
6.	Denomination of Banknotes (INR)	:	5,10,20,50,100,500,1000
7.	Denomination of Coins (INR/ Paise)	:	INR: 1,2,5,10 Paise: 50
8.	Exchange Rate (as of Dec. 2012)	:	54.81

62. INDONESIA

1.	Currency (Currency Code)	:	Indonesian rupiah (IDR)
	Numeric Code	:	360
2.	Subunit	:	1 IDR = 100 sen
3.	Currency Status	:	Floating
4.	Quotation	:	IDR per US dollar
5.	Central Bank (Website)	:	Bank Indonesia (www.bi.go.id)
6.	Denomination of Banknotes (IDR)	:	1000,2000,5000,10000,20000,50000,100000
7.	Denomination of Coins (IDR)	:	100,200,500,1000
8.	Exchange Rate (as of Dec. 2012)	:	9645.00

63. IRAN

1.	Currency (Currency Code)	:	Iranian rial (IRR)
	Numeric Code	:	364
2.	Subunit	:	1 IRR = 100 dinars, 1 toman = 10 IRR
3.	Currency Status	:	Managed float
4.	Quotation	:	IRR per US dollar
5.	Central Bank (Website)	:	Central Bank of the Islamic Republic of Iran (www.cbi.ir)
6.	Denomination of Banknotes (IRR)	:	100, 200, 500, 1000, 20005000, 10000,20000, 50000, 100000
7.	Denomination of Coins (IRR)	:	250, 500, 1000
8.	Exchange Rate (as of Dec. 2012)	:	12,285.00

64. IRAQ

1.	Currency (Currency Code)	:	Iraqi dinar (IQD)
	Numeric Code	:	368
2.	Subunit	:	1 IQD = 1000 fils
3.	Currency Status	:	Managed daily
4.	Quotation	:	IQD per US dollar
5.	Central Bank (Website)	:	Central Bank of Iraq (www.cbi.iq)
6.	Denomination of Banknotes (IDQ)	:	50, 250, 500, 1000, 5000, 10000, 25000
7.	Denomination of Coins (IDQ)	:	Not used
8.	Exchange Rate (as of Dec. 2012)	:	1163.00

65. ISRAEL

1.	Currency (Currency Code)	:	Israeli shekel (ILS)
	Numeric Code	:	376
2.	Subunit	:	1 ILS = 100 agorot
3.	Currency Status	:	Free-floating
4.	Quotation	:	ILS per US dollar
5.	Central Bank (Website)	:	Bank of Israel (www.bankisrael.gov.il)
6.	Denomination of Banknotes (ILS)	:	20,50,100,200
7.	Denomination of Coins (ILS/ Agorot)	:	ILS: .5,1,2,5,10 Agorot: 10
8.	Exchange Rate (as of Dec. 2012)	:	3.73

66. JAMAICA

1.	Currency (Currency Code)	:	Jamaican dollar (JMD)
	Numeric Code	:	388
2.	Subunit	:	1 JMD = 100 cents
3.	Currency Status	:	Floating, crawl-like
4.	Quotation	:	JMD per US dollar
5.	Central Bank (Website)	:	Bank of Jamaica (www.boj.org.jm)
6.	Denomination of Banknotes (JMD)	:	50,100,500,1000
7.	Denomination of Coins (JMD/ Cents)	:	JMD: 1,5,10,20 Cents: 25
8.	Exchange Rate (as of Dec. 2012)	:	92.17

67. JAPAN

1.	Currency (Currency Code)	:	Japanese yen (JPY)
	Numeric Code	:	392
2.	Subunit	:	1 JPY = 100 sen
3.	Currency Status	:	Free-floating
4.	Quotation	:	JPY per US dollar
5.	Central Bank (Website)	:	Bank of Japan (www.boj.or.jp)
6.	Denomination of Banknotes (JPY)	:	1000,2000,5000,10000
7.	Denomination of Coins (JPY)	:	1,5,10,50,100,500
8.	Exchange Rate (as of Dec. 2012)	:	92.00

68. JORDAN

1.	Currency (Currency Code)	:	Jordanian dinar (JOD)
	Numeric Code	:	400
2.	Subunit	:	1 JOD =10 dirham, 1 JOD = 100 piastres, 1 JOD = 1000 fils
3.	Currency Status	:	Pegged to the US dollar (0.71:1)
4.	Quotation	:	JOD per US dollar
5.	Central Bank (Website)	:	Central Bank of Jordan (www.cbj.gov.jo)
6.	Denomination of Banknotes (JOD)	:	1,5,10,20,50
7.	Denomination of Coins (JOD/ Piastres)	:	JOD: .25,.5 Piastres: 1,5,10
8.	Exchange Rate (as of Dec. 2012)	:	0.71

69. KAZAKHSTAN

1.	Currency (Currency Code)	:	Kazakstani tenge (KZT)
	Numeric Code	:	398
2.	Subunit	:	1 KZT = 100 tein
3.	Currency Status	:	Managed float
4.	Quotation	:	KZT per US dollar
5.	Central Bank (Website)	:	National Bank of Kazakhstan (www.nationalbank.kz)
6.	Denomination of Banknotes (KZT)	:	200, 500, 1000, 2000, 5000, 10000
7.	Denomination of Coins (KZT)	:	1,2,5,10,20,50,100
8.	Exchange Rate (as of Dec. 2012)	:	150.11

70. KENYA

1.	Currency (Currency Code)	:	Kenyan shilling (KES)
	Numeric Code	:	404
2.	Subunit	:	1 KES = 100 cents
3.	Currency Status	:	Managed float
4.	Quotation	:	KES per US dollar
5.	Central Bank (Website)	:	Central Bank of Kenya (www.centralbank.go.ke)
6.	Denomination of Banknotes (KES)	:	50, 100, 200, 500, 1000
7.	Denomination of Coins (KES)	:	1,5,10,20
8.	Exchange Rate (as of Dec. 2012)	:	85.91

71. KOREA (NORTH KOREA)

1.	Currency (Currency Code)	:	North Korean won (KPW)
	Numeric Code	:	
2.	Subunit	:	1 KPW = 100 chon
3.	Currency Status	:	Floating
4.	Quotation	:	KPW per US dollar
5.	Central Bank	:	Central Bank of the Democratic People's Republic of Korea
6.	Denomination of Banknotes (KPW)	:	5, 10, 50, 100, 200, 500, 1000, 2000, 5000
7.	Denomination of Coins (KPW)	:	1, 5, 10, 50
8.	Exchange Rate (as of Dec. 2012)	:	128.20

72. KOREA (REPUBLIC OF SOUTH KOREA)

1.	Currency (Currency Code)	:	South Korean won (KRW)
	Numeric Code	:	410
2.	Subunit	:	1 KRW = 100 jeon
3.	Currency Status	:	Managed float
4.	Quotation	:	KRW per US dollar
5.	Central Bank (Website)	:	The Bank of Korea (www.bok.or.kr)
6.	Denomination of Banknotes (KRW)	:	1000,5000,10000,50000
7.	Denomination of Coins (KRW)	:	1,5,10,50,100,500
8.	Exchange Rate (as of Dec. 2012)	:	1062.87

73. KUWAIT

1.	Currency (Currency Code)	:	Kuwaiti dinar (KWD)
	Numeric Code	:	414
2.	Subunit	:	1 KWD = 1000 fils
3.	Currency Status	:	Pegged to a basket of currencies
4.	Quotation	:	KWD per US dollar
5.	Central Bank (Website)	:	Central Bank of Kuwait (www.cbk,gov.kw)
6.	Denomination of Banknotes (KWD)	:	¼,½,1,5,10,20
7.	Denomination of Coins (KWD)	:	Fils: 5,10,20,50,100
8.	Exchange Rate (as of Dec. 2012)	:	0.281

74. KYRGYZSTAN (THE KYRGYZ REPUBLIC)

1.	Currency (Currency Code)	:	Kyrgyz som (KGS)
	Numeric Code	:	417
2.	Subunit	:	1 KGS = 100 tyiyns
3.	Currency Status	:	Managed float
4.	Quotation	:	KGS per US dollar
5.	Central Bank (Website)	:	National Bank of the Kyrgyz Republic (www.nbkr.kg)
6.	Denomination of Banknotes (KGS)	:	20,50,100,200,500,1000,5000
7.	Denomination of Coins (KGS)	:	1,3,5,10
8.	Exchange Rate (as of Dec. 2012)	:	47.40

75. LAO

1.	Currency (Currency Code)	:	Laotian kip (LAK)
	Numeric Code	:	418
2.	Subunit	:	1 LAK = 100 cents
3.	Currency Status	:	Managed float
4.	Quotation	:	LAK per US dollar
5.	Central Bank (Website)	:	Bank of the Lao P.D.R. (www.bol.gov.la)
6.	Denomination of Banknotes (LAK)	:	500, 1000, 2000, 5000, 10000, 20000, 50000, 100000
7.	Denomination of Coins (Cents)	:	Rarely used
8.	Exchange Rate (as of Dec. 2012)	:	7965.50

76. LATVIA

1.	Currency (Currency Code)	:	Latvian lats (LVL) (Note: LVL is scheduled to be replaced by the euro on 1 January 2014.)
	Numeric Code	:	
			428
2.	Subunit	:	1 LVL = 100 santimi
3.	Currency Status	:	Pegged to the euro (0.70:1)
4.	Quotation	:	LVL per US dollar
5.	Central Bank (Website)	:	Bank of Latvia (www.bank.lv)
6.	Denomination of Banknotes (LVL)	:	5,10,20,50,100,500
7.	Denomination of Coins (LVL/ Santim)	:	LVL: 1,2 Santim: 1,2,5,10,20,50
8.	Exchange Rate (as of Dec. 2012)	:	0.53

77. LEBANON

1.	Currency (Currency Code)	:	Lebanese pound (LBP)
	Numeric Code	:	422
2.	Subunit	:	1 LBP = 100 piastre
3.	Currency Status	:	Pegged to the US dollar
4.	Quotation	:	LBP per US dollar
5.	Central Bank (Website)	:	Banque du Liban (www.bdl.gov.lb)
6.	Denomination of Banknotes (LBP)	:	1000, 5000, 10000, 20000, 50000, 100000
7.	Denomination of Coins (LBP)	:	200,500
8.	Exchange Rate (as of Dec. 2012)	:	1502.31

78. LESOTHO

1.	Currency (Currency Code)	:	Lesotho loti (LSL)
	Numeric Code	:	426
2.	Subunit	:	1 LSL = 100 lisente
3.	Currency Status	:	Pegged to the South African rand
4.	Quotation	:	LSL per US dollar
5.	Central Bank (Website)	:	Central Bank of Lesotho (www.centralbank.org.ls)
6.	Denomination of Banknotes (LSL)	:	10,20,50,100,200
7.	Denomination of Coins (LSL/ lisente))	:	LSL: 1,2,5 Lisente: 1,2,5,10,20,50
8.	Exchange Rate (as of Dec. 2012)	:	8.45

79. LIBERIA

1.	Currency (Currency Code)	:	Liberian dollar (LRD)
	Numeric Code	:	430
2.	Subunit	:	1 LRD = 100 cents
3.	Currency Status	:	Managed
4.	Quotation	:	LRD per US dollar
5.	Central Bank (Website)	:	Central Bank of Liberia (cbl.org.lr)
6.	Denomination of Banknotes (LRD)	:	5,10,20,50,100
7.	Denomination of Coins (LRD/ Cents)	:	LRD: 1 Cents: 5,10,25,50
8.	Exchange Rate (as of Dec. 2012)	:	72.50

80. LIBYA

1.	Currency (Currency Code) Numeric Code	: :	Libyan dinar (LYD) 434
2.	Subunit	:	1 LYD = 1000 dirhams
3.	Currency Status	:	Pegged to a basket of currencies
4.	Quotation	:	LYD per US dollar
5.	Central Bank (Website)	:	Central Bank of Libya (www.cbl.gov.ly)
6.	Denomination of Banknotes (LYD)	:	1,5,10,20,50
7.	Denomination of Coins (LYD/ Dirham)	:	LYD: .25,.5 Dirham: 50,100
8.	Exchange Rate (as of Dec. 2012)	:	1.26

81. LITHUANIA

1.	Currency (Currency Code) Numeric Code	: :	Lithuanian litas (LTL) 440
2.	Subunit	:	1 LTL = 100 centas
3.	Currency Status	:	Pegged to the euro
4.	Quotation	:	Fixed exchange system
5.	Central Bank (Website)	:	Central Bank of the Republic of Lithuania (www.lb.lt)
6.	Denomination of Banknotes (LTL)	:	10,20,50,100,200,500
7.	Denomination of Coins (LTL/ Centas)	:	LTL: 1,2,5 Centas: 1,2,5,10,20,50
8.	Exchange Rate History(LTL per EUR,as of Dec. 2012)	:	3.45

82. MACAU

1.	Currency (Currency Code)	:	Macanese pataca (MOP)
	Numeric Code	:	446
2.	Subunit	:	1 MOP = 100 avos
3.	Currency Status	:	Pegged to the Hong Kong dollar
4.	Quotation	:	MOP per US dollar
5.	Central Bank (Website)	:	Monetary Authority of Macau (www.amcm.gov.mo)
6.	Denomination of Banknotes (MOP)	:	10,20,50,100,500,1000
7.	Denomination of Coins (MOP/Avos)	:	MOP: 5 Avos: 10,50
8.	Exchange Rate (as of Dec. 2012)	:	7.98

83. MACEDONIA

1.	Currency (Currency Code)	:	Macedonian denar (MKD)
	Numeric Code	:	807
2.	Subunit	:	1 MKD = 100 deni
3.	Currency Status	:	Managed float
4.	Quotation	:	MKD per US dollar
5.	Central Bank (Website)	:	National Bank of the Republic of Macedonia (www.nbrm.mk)
6.	Denomination of Banknotes (MKD)	:	10, 50, 100, 500, 1000, 5000
7.	Denomination of Coins (MKD)	:	1,2,5,10,50
8.	Exchange Rate (as of Dec. 2012)	:	47.19

84. MADAGASCAR

1.	Currency (Currency Code)	:	Malagasy ariary (MGA)
	Numeric Code	:	969
2.	Subunit	:	1MGA =5 iraimbilanja
3.	Currency Status	:	Free-floating
4.	Quotation	:	MGA per US dollar
5.	Central Bank (Website)	:	Banque Centrale de Madagascar (www.banque-centrale.mg)
6.	Denomination of Banknotes (MGA)	:	100, 200, 500, 1000, 2000, 5000, 10000
7.	Denomination of Coins (MGA/Iraimbilanja)	:	MGA: 2,4,5,10,20,50 Iraimbilanja: 1,2
8.	Exchange Rate (as of Dec. 2012)	:	2247.19

85. MALAWI

1.	Currency (Currency Code)	:	Malawian kwacha (MWK)
	Numeric Code	:	454
2.	Subunit	:	1 MWK = 100 tambala
3.	Currency Status	:	Managed float
4.	Quotation	:	MWK per US dollar
5.	Central Bank (Website)	:	Reserve Bank of Malawi (www.rbm.mw)
6.	Denomination of Banknotes (MWK)	:	20,50,100,200,500,1000
7.	Denomination of Coins (MWK)	:	1,5,10
8.	Exchange Rate (as of Dec. 2012)	:	334.62

86. MALAYSIA

1.	Currency (Currency Code)	:	Malaysian ringgit (MYR)
	Numeric Code	:	458
2.	Subunit	:	1 MYR = 100 sen
3.	Currency Status	:	Managed float
4.	Quotation	:	MYR per US dollar
5.	Central Bank (Website)	:	Bank Negara Malaysia (www.bnm.gov.my)
6.	Denomination of Banknotes (MYR)	:	1,5,10,20,50,100
7.	Denomination of Coins (MYR)	:	5,10,20,50
8.	Exchange Rate (as of Dec. 2012)	:	3.05

87. MALDIVES

1.	Currency (Currency Code)	:	Maldivian rufiyaa (MVR)
	Numeric	:	462
2.	Subunit	:	1 MVR = 100 laari
3.	Currency Status	:	Managed float
4.	Quotation	:	MVR per US dollar
5.	Central Bank (Website)	:	Maldives Monetary Authority (www.mma.gov.mv)
6.	Denomination of Banknotes (MVR)	:	5,10,20,50,100,500
7.	Denomination of Coins (MVR/Laari)	:	Laari: 1,5,10,25,50 MVR: 1,2
8.	Exchange Rate (as of Dec. 2012)	:	15.32

88. MAURITANIA

1.	Currency (Currency Code)	:	Mauritanian ouguiya (MRO)
	Numeric	:	478
2.	Subunit	:	1 MRO = 5 khoums
3.	Currency Status	:	Managed float
4.	Quotation	:	MRO per US dollar
5.	Central Bank (Website)	:	Banque Centrale de Mauritanie (www.bcm.mr)
6.	Denomination of Banknotes (MRO)	:	100,200,500,1000,2000,5000
7.	Denomination of Coins (MRO)	:	5,10,20,50
8.	Exchange Rate (as of Dec. 2012)	:	302.52

89. MAURITIUS

1.	Currency (Currency Code)	:	Mauritian rupee (MUR)
	Numeric Code	:	480
2.	Subunit	:	1 MUR = 100 cents
3.	Currency Status	:	Managed float
4.	Quotation	:	MUR per US dollar
5.	Central Bank (Website)	:	Bank of Mauritius (www.bom.mu)
6.	Denomination of Banknotes (MUR)	:	25, 50, 100, 200, 500, 1000, 2000
7.	Denomination of Coins(MUR)	:	1,5,10,20
8.	Exchange Rate (as of Dec. 2012)	:	30.64

90. MEXICO

1.	Currency (Currency Code)	:	Mexican peso (MXN)
	Numeric Code	:	484
2.	Subunit	:	1 MXN = 100 centavos
3.	Currency Status	:	Independent, free-floating
4.	Quotation	:	MXN per US dollar
5.	Central Bank (Website)	:	Bank of Mexico (www.banxico.org.mx)
6.	Denomination of Banknotes (MXN)	:	20, 50, 100, 200, 500
7.	Denomination of Coins (MXN/Centavos)	:	1,2,5,10 Centavo: 10,20,50
8.	Exchange Rate (as of Dec. 2012)	:	13.00

91. MOLDOVA

1.	Currency (Currency Code)	:	Moldovan leu (MDL)
	Numeric Code	:	498
2.	Subunit	:	1 MDL = 100 bani
3.	Currency Status	:	Floating
4.	Quotation	:	MDL per US dollar
5.	Central Bank (Website)	:	National Bank of Moldova (www.bnm.md)
6.	Denomination of Banknotes (MDL)	:	1, 5, 10, 20, 50, 100, 200, 500, 1000
7.	Denomination of Coins(Bani)	:	1,5,10,25,50
8.	Exchange Rate (as of Dec. 2012)	:	12.04

92. MONGOLIA

1.	Currency (Currency Code)	:	Mongolian togrog (MNT)
	Numeric Code	:	496
2.	Subunit	:	1 MNT = 100 mongo
3.	Currency Status	:	Floating
4.	Quotation	:	MNT per US dollar
5.	Central Bank (Website)	:	Bank of Mongolia (www.mongolbank.mn)
6.	Denomination of Banknotes (MNT)	:	1, 5, 10, 20, 50, 100, 500,1000, 5000, 10000, 20000
7.	Denomination of Coins (MNT)	:	20, 50, 100, 200, 500
8.	Exchange Rate (as of Dec. 2012)	:	1379.49

93. MOROCCO

1.	Currency (Currency Code)	:	Moroccan dirham (MAD)
	Numeric Code	:	504
2.	Subunit	:	1 MAD = 100 santim
3.	Currency Status	:	Pegged to a basket of currencies
4.	Quotation	:	MAD per US dollar
5.	Central Bank (Website)	:	Bank Al-Maghreb (www.bkam.ma)
6.	Denomination of Banknotes (MAD)	:	20,50,100,200
7.	Denomination of Coins (MAD/Santim)	:	MAD: .5,1,2,5,10 Santim: 10,20
8.	Exchange Rate (as of Dec. 2012)	:	8.46

94. MOZAMBIQUE

1.	Currency (Currency Code)	:	Mozambican metical (MZN)
	Numeric Code	:	943
2.	Subunit	:	1MZN = 100 centavo
3.	Currency Status	:	Independent, free-floating
4.	Quotation	:	MZN per US dollar
5.	Central Bank (Website)	:	Banco de Mocambique (www.bancomoc.mz)
6.	Denomination of Banknotes (MZN)	:	20,50,100,200,500,1000
7.	Denomination of Coins (MZN)	:	MZN: 1, 2, 5, 10 Centavo: 1, 5, 10, 20, 50
8.	Exchange Rate (as of Dec. 2012)	:	29.60

95. MYANMAR (BURMA)

1.	Currency (Currency Code)	:	Myanmar kyat (MMK)
	Numeric Code	:	104
2.	Subunit	:	1 MMK = 100 pyas
3.	Currency Status	:	Free float vs US dollar
4.	Quotation	:	MMK per US dollar
5.	Central Bank (Website)	:	Central Bank of Myanmar (www.cbm.gov.mm)
6.	Denomination of Banknotes (MMK)	:	MMK:1, 5, 10, 20, 50, 100, 200, 500, 1000, 000, 10000 Pyas: 50
7.	Denomination of Coins (MMK/Pyas)	:	Pyas: 1,5,10,25,50 MMK: 1,5,10,50,100
8.	Exchange Rate (as of Dec. 2012)	:	857.50

96. NAMIBIA

1.	Currency (Currency Code)	:	Namibian dollar (NAD)
	Numeric Code	:	516
2.	Subunit	:	1 NAD = 100 cents
3.	Currency Status	:	On par with the South African rand
4.	Quotation	:	NAD per US dollar
5.	Central Bank (Website)	:	Bank of Namibia (www.bon.com.na)
6.	Denomination of Banknotes (NAD)	:	10, 20, 50, 100, 200
7.	Denomination of Coins (NAD/Cents)	:	NAD: 1,5,10 Cents: 5,10,50
8.	Exchange Rate (as of Dec. 2012)	:	8.47

97. NEPAL

1.	Currency (Currency Code)	:	Nepalese rupee (NPR)
	Numeric Code	:	524
2.	Subunit	:	1 NPR = 100 paisa
3.	Currency Status	:	Pegged to the Indian rupee
4.	Quotation	:	NPR per US dollar
5.	Central Bank (Website)	:	Nepal Rastra Bank (www.nrb.org.np)
6.	Denomination of Banknotes (NPR)	:	5,10,25,50,100,500,1000
7.	Denomination of Coins (NPR/ Paise)	:	NPR: 1,2,5,10 Paise: 1,5,10,25,50
8.	Exchange Rate (as of Dec. 2012)	:	87.89

98. NETHERELANDS ANTILLES

1.	Currency (Currency Code) Numeric Code	: :	Netherlands Antillean guilder (ANG) 532
2.	Subunit	:	1 ANG = 100 cents
3.	Currency Status	:	Pegged to the US dollar
4.	Quotation	:	ANG per US dollar
5.	Central Bank (Website)	:	Central Bank of Curacao and Sint Maarten (www.centralbank.an)
6.	Denomination of Banknotes (ANG)	:	10,25,50,100
7.	Denomination of Coins (ANG/Cents)	:	ANG: 1,2.5,5 Cents: 1,5,10,25,50,
8.	Exchange Rate (as of Dec. 2012)	:	1.79

99. NEW ZEALAND

1.	Currency (Currency Code) Numeric Code	: :	New Zealand dollar (NZD) 554
2.	Subunit	:	1 NZD = 100 cents
3.	Currency Status	:	free-floating
4.	Quotation	:	US dollar per NZD
5.	Central Bank (Website)	:	Reserve Bank of New Zealand (www.rbnz.govt.nz)
6.	Denomination of Banknotes (NZD)	:	5,10,20,50,100

| 7. | Denomination of Coins (NZD/Cents) | : | NZD: 1,2
 Cents: 10,20,50 |
| 8. | Exchange Rate (USD per NZD, as of Dec. 2012) | : | 0.83 |

100. NICARAGUA

1.	Currency (Currency Code)	:	Nicaraguan cordoba (NIO)
	Numeric Code	:	558
2.	Subunit	:	1 NIO = 100 centavos
3.	Currency Status	:	Managed float
4.	Quotation	:	NIO per US dollar
5.	Central Bank (Website)	:	Central Bank of Nicaragua (www.bcn.gob.ni)
6.	Denomination of Banknotes (NIO)	:	10,20,50,100,200,500
7.	Denomination of Coins (NIO/ Centavo)	:	Centavo: 5,10,25,50 NIO: 1,5,10
8.	Exchange Rate (as of Dec. 2012)	:	24.10

101. NIGERIA

1.	Currency (Currency Code)	:	Nigerian naira (NGN)
	Numeric Code	:	566
2.	Subunit	:	1 NGN = 100 kobo
3.	Currency Status	:	Managed float
4.	Quotation	:	NGN per US dollar
5.	Central Bank (Website)	:	Central Bank of Nigeria (www.cenbank.org)

6.	Denomination of Banknotes (NGN)	:	5,10,20,50,100,200,500,1000
7.	Denomination of Coins (NGN/Kobo)	:	Kobo: 50 NGN: 1,2
8.	Exchange Rate (as of Dec. 2012)	:	156.15

102. NORWAY

1.	Currency (Currency Code) Numeric Code	: :	Norwegian krone (NOK) 578
2.	Subunit	:	1 NOK = 100 ore
3.	Currency Status	:	Floating
4.	Quotation	:	NOK per US dollar
5.	Central Bank (Website)	:	Norgesbank (www.norges-bank.no)
6.	Denomination of Banknotes (NOK)	:	50,100,200,500
7.	Denomination of Coins (NOK)	:	1,5,10,20
8.	Exchange Rate (as of Dec. 2012)	:	5.58

103. OMAN

1.	Currency (Currency Code) Numeric Code	: :	Omani rial (OMR) 512
2.	Subunit	:	1 OMR = 1000 baisa
3.	Currency Status	:	Pegged to the US dollar
4.	Quotation	:	OMR per US dollar

5.	Central Bank (Website)	:	Central Bank of Oman (www.cbo-oman.org)
6.	Denomination of Banknotes (OMR)	:	Baisa:100,200,500 OMR:, ½,1,5,10,20,50
7.	Denomination of Coins (Baisa)	:	5,10,25,50
8.	Exchange Rate (as of Dec. 2012)	:	0.380

104. PAKISTAN

1.	Currency (Currency Code) Numeric Code	: :	Pakistani rupee (PKR) 586
2.	Subunit	:	1 PKR = 100 paisa
3.	Currency Status	:	Managed float
4.	Quotation	:	PKR per US dollar
5.	Central Bank (Website)	:	State Bank of Pakistan (www.sbp.org.pk)
6.	Denomination of Banknotes (PKR)	:	10,50,100,500,1000
7.	Denomination of Coins (PKR)	:	1,2,5
8.	Exchange Rate (as of Dec. 2012)	:	97.35

105. PANAMA

1.	Currency (Currency Code) Numeric Code	: :	Panamanian balboa (PAB) 590
2.	Subunit	:	1 PAB = 100 centesimo
3.	Currency Status	:	Pegged to US dollar (1:1)
4.	Quotation	:	PAB per US dollar

5.	Central Bank (Website)	:	National Bank of Panama (www.banconal.com.pa)
6.	Denomination of Banknotes (PAB)	:	None (US dollar notes used)
7.	Denomination of Coins (PAB/ Centesimo)	:	Centesimo: 1,5 PAB: .1,.25,.5,1,2
8.	Exchange Rate	:	Pegged to US dollar at par.

106. PAPUA NEW GUINEA

1.	Currency (Currency Code) Numeric Code	: :	Papua New Guinean kina (PGK) 598
2.	Subunit	:	1 PGK = 100 toea
3.	Currency Status	:	Floating
4.	Quotation	:	US dollar per PGK
5.	Central Bank (Website)	:	Bank of Papua New Guinea (www.bankpng.gov.pg)
6.	Denomination of Banknotes (PGK)	:	2,5,10,20,50,100
7.	Denomination of Coins (PGK/ Toea)	:	Toea: 5,10,20,50 PJK: 1
8.	Exchange Rate (USD per PGK, as of Dec. 2012)	:	0.48

107. PARAGUAY

1.	Currency (Currency Code) Numeric Code	: :	Paraguayan guarani (PYG) 600
2.	Subunit	:	1 PYG = 100 centimas
3.	Currency Status	:	Managed float
4.	Quotation	:	PYG per US dollar

5.	Central Bank (Website)	:	Banco Central del Paraguay (www.bcp.gov.py)
6.	Denomination of Banknotes (PYG)	:	2000,5000,10000,20000,50000, 100000
7.	Denomination of Coins (PYG)	:	50,100,500,1000
8.	Exchange Rate (as of Dec. 2012)	:	4274.96

108. PERU

1.	Currency (Currency Code)	:	Peruvian nuevo sol (PEN)
	Numeric Code	:	604
2.	Subunit	:	1 PEN = 100 centimos
3.	Currency Status	:	Floating
4.	Quotation	:	PEN per US dollar
5.	Central Bank (Website)	:	Central Reserve Bank of Peru (www.bcrp.gob.pe)
6.	Denomination of Banknotes (PEN)	:	10,20,50,100
7.	Denomination of Coins (PEN/ Centimos)	:	Centimos: 10,20,50 PEN: 1,2,5
8.	Exchange Rate (as of Dec. 2012)	:	2.55

109. PHILIPPINES

1.	Currency (Currency Code)	:	Philippine peso (PHP)
	Numeric ocde	:	608
2.	Subunit	:	1 PHP = 100 sentimo
3.	Currency Status	:	Floating
4.	Quotation	:	PHP per US dollar

5.	Central Bank (Website)	:	Bangko Sentral ng pilipinas (www.bsp.gov.ph)
6.	Denomination of Banknotes (PHP)	:	20,50,100,200,500,1000
7.	Denomination of Coins (PHP/ Sentimo)	:	Sentimo: 25 PHP: 1,5,10
8.	Exchange Rate (as of Dec. 2012)	:	41.08

110. POLAND

1.	Currency (Currency Code) Numeric Code	: :	Polish zloty (PLN) 985
2.	Subunit	:	1 PLN = 100 grosz
3.	Currency Status	:	Free-floating
4.	Quotation	:	PLN per US dollar
5.	Central Bank (Website)	:	National Bank of Poland (www.nbp.pl)
6.	Denomination of Banknotes (PLN)	:	10,20,50,100,200
7.	Denomination of Coins (PLN/ Grosz)	:	Grosz: 1,2,5,10,20,50 PLN: 1,2,5
8.	Exchange Rate (as of Dec. 2012)	:	3.08

111. QATAR

1.	Currency (Currency Code) Numeric Code	: :	Qatari riyal (QAR) 634
2.	Subunit	:	1 QAR = 100 dirhams
3.	Currency Status	:	Pegged to the US dollar

4.	Quotation	:	QAR per US dollar
5.	Central Bank (Website)	:	Qatar Central Bank (www.qcb.gov.qa)
6.	Denomination of Banknotes (QAR)	:	1,5,10,50,100,500
7.	Denomination of Coins (Dirham)	:	Dirham: 1,5,10,25,50
8.	Exchange Rate (as of Dec. 2012)	:	3.64

112. ROMANIA

1.	Currency (Currency Code)	:	Romanian leu (RON)
	Numeric Code	:	946
2.	Subunit	:	1 RON = 100 bani
3.	Currency Status	:	Managed float
4.	Quotation	:	RON per US dollar
5.	Central Bank (Website)	:	National Bank of Romania (www.bnro.ro)
6.	Denomination of Banknotes (RON)	:	1,5,10,50,100
7.	Denomination of Coins (RON/Bani)	:	Bani: 10,50 RON: 1
8.	Exchange Rate (as of Dec. 2012)	:	3.36

113. RUSSIAN FEDERATION

1.	Currency (Currency Code)	:	Russian ruble (RUB)
	Numeric Code	:	643
2.	Subunit	:	1 RUB = 100 kopeks

3.	Currency Status	:	Managed float
4.	Quotation	:	RUB per US dollar
5.	Central Bank (Website)	:	Bank of Russia (www.cbr.ru)
6.	Day Count Convention	:	Actual/365
7.	Denomination of Banknotes (RUB)	:	50,100,500,1000
8.	Denomination of Coins (RUB/ Kopeks)	:	Kopeks: 10,50 RUB: 1,2,5,10,25
9.	Exchange Rate (as of Dec. 2012)	:	30.37

114. RWANDA

1.	Currency (Currency Code)	:	Rwandan franc (RWF)
	Numeric Code	:	646
2.	Subunit	:	1 RWF = 100 centimes
3.	Currency Status	:	Crawl-like arrangement
4.	Quotation	:	RWF per US dollar
5.	Central Bank (Website)	:	National Bank of Rwanda (www.bnr.rw)
6.	Denomination of Banknotes (RWF)	:	100,500,1000,5000
7.	Denomination of Coins (RWF)	:	1,5,10,20,50,100
8.	Exchange Rate (as of Dec. 2012)	:	624.00

115. SAINT HELENA

1.	Currency (Currency Code)	:	Saint Helena pound (SHP)
	Numeric Code	:	654
2.	Subunit	:	1 SHP = 100 penny
3.	Currency Status	:	Pegged to GBP
4.	Quotation	:	US dollar per SHP
5.	Central Bank (Website)	:	Government of Saint Helena (www.sainthelena.gov.sh)
6.	Denomination of Banknotes (SHP)	:	5,10,20
7.	Denomination of Coins (SHP/ Pence)	:	SHP: 1,2 Pence: 1,2,5,10,20,50
8.	Exchange Rate (as of Dec. 2012)	:	1.62

116. SAMOA (WEST SAMOA)

1.	Currency (Currency Code)	:	Samoan tala (WST)
	Numeric Code	:	882
2.	Subunit	:	1 WST = 100 sene
3.	Currency Status	:	Pegged to a basket of currencies
4.	Quotation	:	US dollar per WST
5.	Central Bank (Website)	:	Central Bank of Samoa (www.cbs.gov.ws)
6.	Denomination of Banknotes (WST)	:	2,5,10,20,50,100
7.	Denomination of Coins (WST/Sene)	:	Sene: 10,20,50 WST: 1,2
8.	Exchange Rate (as of Dec. 2012)	:	2.26

117. SAO TOME AND PRINCIPE

1.	Currency (Currency Code) Numeric Code	: :	Sao Tome and Principe dobra (STD) 678
2.	Subunit	:	1 STD = 100 centimos
3.	Currency Status	:	Linked to the euro (24,000:1)
4.	Quotation	:	STD per US dollar
5.	Central Bank (Website)	:	Banco Central de Sao Tome e Principe (www.bcstp.st)
6.	Denomination of Banknotes (STD)	:	5000, 10000, 20000, 50000, 100000
7.	Denomination of Coins (STD)	:	100,250,500,1000,2000
8.	Exchange Rate (as of Dec. 2012)	:	18570.00

118. SAUDI ARABIA

1.	Currency (Currency Code) Numeric Code	: :	Saudi riyal (SAR) 682
2.	Subunit	:	1 SAR = 100 halalah
3.	Currency Status	:	Pegged to the US dollar
4.	Quotation	:	SAR per US dollar
5.	Central Bank (Website)	:	Saudi Arabian Monetary Agency (www.sama.gov.sa)
6.	Denomination of Banknotes (SAR)	:	1,5,10,20,50,100,500
7.	Denomination of Coins (Halalah)	:	5,10,25,50,100
8.	Exchange Rate (as of Dec. 2012)	:	3.75

119. SERBIA

1.	Currency (Currency Code)	:	Serbian dinar (RSD)
	Numeric Code	:	941
2.	Subunit	:	1RSD= 100 para
3.	Currency Status	:	Floating
4.	Quotation	:	RSD per US dollar
5.	Central Bank (Website)	:	National Bank of Serbia (www.nbs.rs)
6.	Denomination of Banknotes (RSD)	:	50,100,200,500,1000,2000
7.	Denomination of Coins (RSD)	:	1,2,5,10,20
8	Exchange Rate (as of Dec. 2012)	:	85.85

120. SEYCHELLES

1.	Currency (Currency Code)	:	Seychellois rupee (SCR)
	Numeric Code	:	690
2.	Subunit	:	1 SCR = 100 cents
3.	Currency Status	:	Floating
4.	Quotation	:	SCR per US dollar
5.	Central Bank (Website)	:	Central Bank of Seychelles (www.cbs.sc)
6.	Denomination of Banknotes (SCR)	:	50,100,500
7.	Denomination of Coins (SCR/ Cents)	:	SCR: 1,5 Cents: 1,5,10,25
8.	Exchange Rate (as of Dec. 2012)	:	12.94

121. SIERRA LEONE

1.	Currency (Currency Code)	:	Sierra Leonean leone (SLL)
	Numeric Code	:	694
2.	Subunit	:	1 SLL = 100 cents
3.	Currency Status	:	Floating
4.	Quotation	:	SLL per US dollar
5.	Central Bank (Website)	:	Bank of Sierra Leone (www.bsl.gov.sl)
6.	Denomination of Banknotes (SLL)	:	1000,2000,5000,10000
7.	Denomination of Coins (SLL)	:	10,50,100,500
8.	Exchange Rate (as of Dec. 2012)	:	4330.00

122. SINGAPORE

1.	Currency (Currency Code)	:	Singapore dollar (SGD)
	Numeric Code	:	702
2.	Subunit	:	1 SGD = 100 cents
3.	Currency Status	:	Managed float
4.	Quotation	:	SGD per US dollar
5.	Central Bank (Website)	:	Monetary Authority of Singapore (www.mas.gov.sg)
6.	Denomination of Banknotes (SGD)	:	2, 5, 10, 50, 100, 1000
7.	Denomination of Coins (SGD/ Cents)	:	Cents: 5,10,20,50 SGD: 1
8.	Exchange Rate (as of Dec. 2012)	:	1.22

123. SOLOMON ISLANDS

1.	Currency (Currency Code) Numeric Code	: :	Solomon Islands dollar (SBD) 090
2.	Subunit	:	1 SBD = 100 cents
3.	Currency Status	:	Managed float
4.	Quotation	:	SBD per US dollar
5.	Central Bank (Website)	:	Central Bank of Solomon Islands (www.cbsi.com.sb)
6.	Denomination of Banknotes (SBD)	:	5,10,20,50,100
7.	Denomination of Coins (SBD/ Cents)	:	Cents: 10,20,50 SBD: 1,2
8.	Exchange Rate (as of Dec. 2012)	:	6.97

124. SOMALIA

1.	Currency (Currency Code) Numeric Code	: :	Somali shilling (SOS) 706
2.	Subunit	:	1 SOS = 100 senti
3.	Currency Status	:	Floating
4.	Quotation	:	SOS per US dollar
5.	Central Bank (Website)	:	Central Bank of Somalia (www.centralbank.so)
6.	Denomination of Banknotes (SOS)	:	5,10,20,50,100
7.	Denomination of Coins (SOS/ Senti)	:	Senti: 1,5,10,50,100 SOS: 1,5,10,50
8.	Exchange Rate (as of Dec. 2012)	:	1605.00

125. SOUTH AFRICA

1.	Currency (Currency Code)	:	South African rand (ZAR)
	Numeric Code	:	710
2.	Subunit	:	1 ZAR = 100 cents
3.	Currency Status	:	Floating
4.	Quotation	:	ZAR per US dollar
5.	Central Bank (Website)	:	South African Reserve Bank (www.reservebank.co.za)
6.	Denomination of Banknotes (ZAR)	:	10, 20, 50, 100, 200
7.	Denomination of Coins (ZAR/ Cents)	:	Cents: 5,10,20,50 ZAR: 1,2,5
8.	Exchange Rate (as of Dec. 2012)	:	8.47

126. SOUTH SUDAN

1.	Currency (Currency Code)	:	South Sudanese pound
	Numeric Code	:	(SSP)
			728
2.	Subunit	:	1 SSP = 100 piaster
3.	Currency Status	:	Managed float
4.	Quotation	:	SSP per USD
5.	Central Bank (Website)	:	Bank of South Sudan (www. bankofsouthern sudan.org)
6.	Denomination of Banknotes (SSP/ Piaster)	:	Piaster: 5,10,25 SSP: 1,5,10,25,50,100
7.	Denomination of Coins (Piaster)	:	Piaster: 1,5,10,25,50
8.	Exchange Rate (as of Dec. 2012)	:	Official: 2.95, Market rate: 4.25

127. SRI LANKA

1.	Currency (Currency Code)	:	Sri Lankan rupee (LKR)
	Numeric Code	:	144
2.	Subunit	:	1 LKR = 100 cents
3.	Currency Status	:	Managed float
4.	Quotation	:	LKR per US dollar
5.	Central Bank (Website)	:	Central Bank of Sri Lanka (www. cbsl.gov.lk)
6.	Denomination of Banknotes (LKR)	:	10,20,50,100,500,1000,2000
7.	Denomination of Coins (LKR/ Cents)	:	Cents: 1,2,5,10,25,50 LKR: 1,2,5,10
8.	Exchange Rate (as of Dec. 2012)	:	126.96

128. SUDAN

1.	Currency (Currency Code)	:	New Sudanese pound (SDG)
	Numeric Code	:	938
2.	Subunit	:	1 SDG = 100 qish (piastres)
3.	Currency Status	:	Managed
4.	Quotation	:	SDG per US dollar
5.	Central Bank (Website)	:	Central Bank of Sudan (www.cbos.gov.sd)
6.	Denomination of Banknotes (SDG)	:	1,2,5,10,20,50
7.	Denomination of Coins (SDG/ Piastres)	:	Piastres: 1,5,10,20,50 SDG: 1
8.	Exchange Rate (as of Dec. 2012)	:	4.41

129. SURINAME

1.	Currency (Currency Code)	:	Surinamese dollar (SRD)
	Numeric Code	:	968
2.	Subunit	:	1 SRD = 100 cents
3.	Currency Status	:	Managed float
4.	Quotation	:	SRD per US dollar
5.	Central Bank (Website)	:	Central Bank of Suriname (www.cbvs.sr)
6.	Denomination of Banknotes (SRD)	:	1,2.5, 5,10,20,50,100
7.	Denomination of Coins (Cents)	:	Cents: 1,5,10,25,100,200
8.	Exchange Rate (as of Dec. 2012)	:	3.28

130. SWAZILAND

1.	Currency (Currency Code)	:	Swaziland lilangeni (SZL)
	Numeric Code	:	748
2.	Subunit	:	1 SZL = 100 cents
3.	Currency Status	:	Pegged to the South African rand
4.	Quotation	:	SZL per US dollar
5.	Central Bank (Website)	:	Central Bank of Swaziland (www.centralbank.org.sz)
6.	Denomination of Banknotes (SZL)	:	10,20,50,100,200
7.	Denomination of Coins (SZL/ Cents)	:	Cents: 1,2,5,10,20,50 SZL: 1,2,5
8.	Exchange Rate (as of Dec. 2012)	:	8.47

131. SWEDEN

1.	Currency (Currency Code)	:	Swedish krona (SEK)
	Numeric Code	;	752
2.	Subunit	:	1 SEK = 100 oren (Note: these subunits have been discontinued.)
3.	Currency Status	:	Free-floating
4.	Quotation	:	SEK per US Dollar
5.	Central Bank (Website)	:	Sveriges Riksbank (www.riksbank.se)
6.	Denomination of Banknotes (SEK)	:	20,50,100,500
7.	Denomination of Coins (SEK)	:	1,5,10
8.	Exchange Rate (as of Dec. 2012)	:	6.50

132. SWITZERLAND

1.	Currency (Currency Code)	:	Swiss franc (CHF)
	Numeric Code	:	756
2.	Subunit	:	1 CHF = 100 centimes/ rappen/centensimo/ rap
3.	Currency Status	:	Managed float
4.	Quotation	:	US dollar per CHF
5.	Central Bank (Website)	:	Swiss National Bank (www. snb.ch)
6.	Denomination of Banknotes (CHF)	:	10,20,50,100,200,1000
7.	Denomination of Coins (CHF/ Centimes)	:	Centimes: 5,10,20 CHF: .5,1,2,5
8.	Exchange Rate (USD per CHF, as of Dec. 2012)	:	1.09
9.	Countries using CHF as Currency	:	Liechtenstein

133. SYRIA

1.	Currency (Currency Code)	:	Syrian pound (SYP)
	Numeric Code	:	760
2.	Subunit	:	1 SYP = 100 piastres
3.	Currency Status	:	Pegged to a basket of currencies
4.	Quotation	:	SYP per US dollar
5.	Central Bank (Website)	:	Central Bank of Syria (www.banquecentrale.gov.sy)
6.	Denomination of Banknotes (SYP)	:	50,100,200,500,1000
7.	Denomination of Coins (SYP)	:	1,2,5,10,25
8.	Exchange Rate (as of Dec. 2012)	:	70.99

134. TAIWAN

1.	Currency (Currency Code)	:	New Taiwan dollar (TWD)
	Numeric Code	:	901
2.	Subunit	:	1 TWD = 100 cents
3.	Currency Status	:	Managed float
4.	Quotation	:	TWD per US dollar
5.	Central Bank (Website)	:	Central Bank of the Republic of China (www.cbc.gov.tw)
6.	Denomination of Banknotes (TWD)	:	100, 500, 1000
7.	Denomination of Coins (TWD)	:	1,5,10,50
8.	Exchange Rate (as of Dec. 2012)	:	29.02

135. TAJIKISTAN

1.	Currency (Currency Code)	:	Tajikistani somoni (TJS)
	Numeric Code	:	972
2.	Subunit	:	1TJS = 100 dirham
3.	Currency Status	:	Managed float
4.	Quotation	:	TJS per US dollar
5.	Central Bank (Website)	:	National Bank of Tajikistan (www.nbt.tj/en)
6.	Denomination of Banknotes (TJS/Dirham)	:	Dirham: 1,5,20,50 TJS: 1, 3, 5, 10, 20, 50, 100, 200, 500
7.	Denomination of Coins (TJS/Dirham)	:	Dirham:1,2, 5,10,20,25,50 TJS: 1,3,5
8.	Exchange Rate (as of Dec. 2012)	:	4.76

136. TANZANIA

1.	Currency (Currency Code)	:	Tanzanian shilling (TZS)
	Numeric Code	:	834
2.	Subunit	:	1 TZS = 100 cents
3.	Currency Status	:	Floating
4.	Quotation	:	TZS per US dollar
5.	Central Bank (Website)	:	Bank of Tanzania (www.bo-tz.org)
6.	Denomination of Banknotes (TZS)	:	500, 1000, 2000, 5000, 10000
7.	Denomination of Coins (TZS/Cents)	:	TZS: 1,5,10,20,50,100,200 Cents: 5,10,20,50
8.	Exchange Rate (as of Dec. 2012)	:	1578.48

137. THAILAND

1.	Currency (Currency Code)	:	Thai baht (THB)
	Numeric Code	:	764
2.	Subunit	:	1 THB = 100 santangs
3.	Currency Status	:	Free-floating
4.	Quotation	:	THB per US dollar
5.	Central Bank (Website)	:	Bank of Thailand (www.bot.or.th)
6.	Day Count Convention	:	Actual/365
7.	Denomination of Banknotes (THB)	:	20,50,100,500,1000
8.	Denomination of Coins (THB/ Santang)	:	Santang: 25,50 THB: 1,2,5,10
9.	Exchange Rate (as of Dec. 2012)	:	30.60

138. TONGA

1.	Currency (Currency Code)	:	Tongan pa'anga (TOP)
	Numeric Code	:	776
2.	Subunit	:	1 TOP = 100 seniti
3.	Currency Status	:	Pegged to a basket of currencies
4.	Quotation	:	TOP per US dollar
5.	Central Bank (Website)	:	National Reserve Bank of Tonga (www.reservebank.to)
6.	Denomination of Banknotes (TOP)	:	1,2,5,10,20,50,100
7.	Denomination of Coins (Seniti)	:	5,10,20,50
8.	Exchange Rate (as of Dec. 2012)	:	1.73

139. TRINIDAD AND TOBAGO

1.	Currency (Currency Code) Numeric Code	: :	Trinidad and Tobago dollar (TTD) 780
2.	Subunit	:	1 TTD = 100 cents
3.	Currency Status	:	Stabilised arrangement
4.	Quotation	:	TTD per US dollar
5.	Central Bank (Website)	:	Central Bank of Trinidad and Tobago (www.central-bank.org.tt)
6.	Denomination of Banknotes (TTD)	:	1,5,10,20,50,100
7.	Denomination of Coins (Cents)	:	1,5,10,25
8.	Exchange Rate (as of Dec. 2012)	:	6.41

140. TUNISIA

1.	Currency (Currency Code) Numeric Code	: :	Tunisian dinar (TND) 788
2.	Subunit	:	1 TND = 1000 millime
3.	Currency Status	:	Managed float
4.	Quotation	:	TND per US dollar
5.	Central Bank (Website)	:	Central Bank of Tunisia (www.bct.gov.tn)
6.	Denomination of Banknotes (TND)	:	10,20,30,50
7.	Denomination of Coins (TND/Millime)	:	Millime: 25,50,100 TND: .5,1,5,
8.	Exchange Rate (as of Dec. 2012)	:	1.56

141. TURKEY

1.	Currency (Currency Code)	:	Turkish lira (TRY)
	Numeric Code	:	949
2.	Subunit	:	1 TRY = 100 kurus
3.	Currency Status	:	Floating
4.	Quotation	:	TRY per US dollar
5.	Central Bank (Website)	:	Central Bank of the Republic of Turkey (www.tcmb.gov.tr)
6.	Denomination of Banknotes (TRY)	:	5,10,20,50,100,200
7.	Denomination of Coins (TRY/ Kurus)	:	Kurus: 5,10,25,50 TRY: 1
8.	Exchange Rate (as of Dec. 2012)	:	1.91

142. TURKMENISTAN

1.	Currency (Currency Code)	:	New Turkmenistan manat (TMT)
	Numeric Code	:	934
2.	Subunit	:	1 TMT = 100 tenge
3.	Currency Status	:	Conventional peg
4.	Quotation	:	TMT per US dollar
5.	Central Bank (Website)	:	Central Bank of Turkmenistan (www.cbt.tm)
6.	Denomination of Banknotes (TMT)	:	1,5,10,20,50,100,500
7.	Denomination of Coins (TMT)	:	Tenge: 1,2,5,10,20,50 TMT: 1,2
8.	Exchange Rate (as of Dec. 2012)	:	2.85

143. UGANDA

1.	Currency (Currency Code)	:	Uganda shilling (UGX)
	Numeric Code	:	800
2.	Subunit	:	1 UGX = 100 cents
3.	Currency Status	:	Floating
4.	Quotation	:	UGX per US dollar
5.	Central Bank (Website)	:	Bank of Uganda (www.bou.or.ug)
6.	Denomination of Banknotes (UGX)	:	1000, 2000, 5000, 10000, 20000, 50000
7.	Denomination of Coins (UGX)	:	100,200,500
8.	Exchange Rate (as of Dec. 2012)	:	2686.00

144. UKRAINE

1.	Currency (Currency Code)	:	Ukrainian hryvnia (UAH)
	Numeric Code	:	980
2.	Subunit	:	1 UAH = 100 kopiyka
3.	Currency Status	:	Managed float
4.	Quotation	:	UAH per US dollar
5.	Central Bank (Website)	:	National Bank of Ukraine (www.bank.gov.ua)
6.	Denomination of Banknotes (UAH)	:	1,2,5,10,20,50,100,200,500
7.	Denomination of Coins (UAH/ Kopiyka)	:	Kopiyka: 1,2,5,10,25,50 UAH: 1
8.	Exchange Rate (as of Dec. 2012)	:	8.04

145. UNITED ARAB EMIRATES (UAE)

1.	Currency (Currency Code)	:	UAE dirham (AED)
	Numeric Code	:	784
2.	Subunit	:	1 AED = 100 fils
3.	Currency Status	:	Pegged to the US dollar
4.	Quotation	:	AED per US dollar
5.	Central Bank (Website)	:	Central Bank of the UAE (www. centralbank.ae)
6.	Denomination of Banknotes (AED)	:	5,10,20,50,100,200,500
7.	Denomination of Coins (AED/ Fils)	:	Fils: 25,50 AED: 1
8.	Exchange Rate (as of Dec. 2012)	:	3.67

146. UNITED KINGDOM

1.	Currency (Currency Code)	:	British pound sterling (GBP)
	Numeric Code	:	826
2.	Subunit	:	1 GBP = 100 pence
3.	Currency Status	:	Free-floating
4.	Quotation	:	US dollar per GBP
5.	Central Bank (Website)	:	Bank of England (www.bankofengland.co.uk)
6.	Denomination of Banknotes (GBP)	:	5,10,20,50
7.	Denomination of Coins (GBP/ Pence)	:	Pence: 1,2,5,10,20,50 GBP: 1,2
8.	Exchange Rate (USD per GBP, as of Dec. 2012)	:	1.62

147. UNITED STATES

1.	Currency (Currency Code)	:	United States dollar (USD)
	Numeric Code	:	840
2.	Subunit	:	1 USD = 100 cents
3.	Currency Status	:	Free-floating
4.	Quotation	:	Foreign currencies per USD, except EUR, GBP, AUD and NZD, which are quoted in USD terms.
5.	Central Bank (Website)	:	Federal Reserve System (www.federalreserve.gov)
6.	Denomination of Banknotes (USD)	:	1,5,10,20,50,100
7.	Denomination of Coins (Cents)	:	1,5,10,25
8.	Countries Using USD as Currency	:	East Timor, El Salvador, Ecuador, Marshall Islands, Micronesia, Palau, Panama Canal Zone, and Puerto Rico.

148. URUGUAY

1.	Currency (Currency Code)	:	Uruguayan peso (UYU)
	Numeric Code	:	858
2.	Subunit	:	1 UYU = 100 centesimos
3.	Currency Status	:	Floating
4.	Quotation	:	UYU per US dollar
5.	Central Bank (Website)	:	Central Bank of Uruguay (www.bcu.gub.uy)
6.	Denomination of Banknotes (UYU)	:	20, 50, 100, 200, 500, 1000, 2000

7..	Denomination of Coins (UYU)	:	1,2,5,10
8	Exchange Rate (as of Dec. 2012)	:	19.15

149. UZBEKISTAN

1.	Currency (Currency Code)	:	Uzbekistani som (UZS)
	Numeric Code	:	860
2.	Subunit	:	1 UZS = 100 tiyin
3.	Currency Status	:	Managed float
4.	Quotation	:	UZS per US dollar
5.	Central Bank (Website)	:	Central Bank of the Republic of Uzbekistan (www.cbu.uz)
6.	Denomination of Banknotes (UZS)	:	1, 3, 5, 10, 25, 50, 100, 200, 500, 1000
7.	Denomination of Coins (UZS)	:	1,5,10,25,50,100
8.	Exchange Rate (as of Dec. 2012)	:	1984.00

150. VANUATU

1.	Currency (Currency Code)	:	Vanuatu vatu (VUV)
	Numeric Code	:	548
2.	Subunit	:	No subdivision
3.	Currency Status	:	Pegged to a basket of currencies
4.	Quotation	:	VUV per US dollar
5.	Central Bank (Website)	:	Reserve Bank of Vanuatu (www.rbv.gov.vu)

6.	Denomination of Banknotes (VUV)	:	100,200,500,1000,5000
7.	Denomination of Coins (VUV)	:	1,2,5,10,20,50,100
8.	Exchange Rate (as of Dec. 2012)	:	91.20

151. VENEZUELA

1.	Currency (Currency Code)	:	Venezuelan bolivar fuerte (VEF)
	Numeric Code	:	937
2.	Subunit	:	1 VEF= 100 centimo
3.	Currency Status	:	Pegged to the US dollar
4.	Quotation	:	VEF per US dollar
5.	Central Bank (Website)	:	Banco Central de Venezuela (www.bcv.org.ve)
6.	Denomination of Banknotes (VEF)	:	2,5,10,20,50,100
7.	Denomination of Coins (VEF/ Centimo)	:	Centimo: 5,10,25,50 VEF: 1
8.	Exchange Rate (as of Dec. 2012)	:	4.30

152. VIETNAM

1.	Currency (Currency Code)	:	Vietnamese dong (VND)
	Numeric Code	:	704
2.	Subunit	:	1 VND = 100 xu
3.	Currency Status	:	Managed float
4.	Quotation	:	VND per US dollar
5.	Central Bank (Website)	:	The State Bank of Vietnam (www.sbv.gov.vn)

6.	Denomination of Banknotes (VND)	:	10000, 20000, 50000, 100000, 200000, 500000
7.	Denomination of Coins (VND)	:	200, 500, 1000, 2000, 5000
8.	Exchange Rate (as of Dec. 2012)	:	20815.00

153. WEST AFRICA USING CFA FRANC

1.	Currency (Currency Code)	:	West African CFA franc (XOF)
	Numeric Code	:	952
2.	Subunit	:	1 XOF = 100 centimes
3.	Currency Status	:	Pegged to the euro (655.96:1)
4.	Quotation	:	XOF per USD
5.	Central Bank (Website)	:	Central Bank of West African States (www.bceao.int)
6.	Denomination of Banknotes (XOF)	:	500, 1000, 2000, 5000, 10000
7.	Denomination of Coins (XOF)	:	1, 5, 10, 25, 50, 100, 200, 250, 500
8.	Exchange Rate (as of Dec. 2012)	:	496.38
9.	Countries Using XOF as Currency	:	Benin, Burkina Faso, Cote d'Ivoire, Guinea Bissau, Mali, Niger, Senegal, and Togo

154. YEMEN

1.	Currency (Currency Code)	:	Yemeni rial (YER)
	Numeric Code	:	886
2.	Subunit	:	1 YER = 100 fils (Note: these are not issued.)

3.	Currency Status	:	Managed float
4.	Quotation	:	YER per US dollar
5.	Central Bank (Website)	:	Central Bank of Yemen (www.centralbank.gov.ye)
6.	Denomination of Banknotes (YER)	:	50, 100, 200, 250, 500, 1000
7.	Denomination of Coins (YER)	:	1,5,10,20
8.	Exchange Rate (as of Dec. 2012)	:	214.05

155. ZAMBIA

1.	Currency (Currency Code) Numeric Code	:	Zambian kwacha (ZMK) (Note: the new code is ZMW) 967
2.	Subunit	:	1 ZMK = 100 ngwee
3.	Currency Status	:	Floating
4.	Quotation	:	ZMK per US dollar
5.	Central Bank (Website)	:	Bank of Zambia (www.boz.zm)
6.	Denomination of Banknotes (ZMK)	:	2,5,10,20,50,100
7.	Denomination of Coins (ZMK/ Ngwee)	:	Ngwee: 5,10,50 ZMK: 1
8.	Exchange Rate (as of Dec. 2012)	:	5235.00

156. ZIMBABWE

1.	Currency (Currency Code)	:	Zimbabwean dollar used to
		:	be the currency of Zimbabwe. It was suspended in 2009. The country now uses a multi-currency regime. Currencies such as South African Rand, Botswana Pula, Pound Sterling, Euro, and United States dollar are now used.
2.	Central Bank (Website)	:	Reserve Bank of Zimbabwe (www.rbz.co.zw)

157. EUROPEAN UNION MEMBERS USING EURO AS CURRENCY

1.	Seventeen Member States of the European Union using EURO	:	Austria
			Belgium
			Cyprus
			Estonia
			Finland
			France
			Germany
			Greece
			Ireland
			Italy
			Luxembourg
			Malta
			Netherlands
			Portugal
			Slovakia
			Slovenia
			Spain

2.	Currency Code	:	European euro (EUR)
	Numeric Code	:	978
3.	Subunit	:	1 EUR = 100 cents
4.	Currency Status	:	Free-floating
5.	Quotation	:	Number of US dollars per euro
6.	Central Bank (Website)	:	European Central Bank (www.ecb.int)
7.	Denomination of Banknotes (EUR)	:	5,10,20,50,100,200,500
8.	Denomination of Coins (EUR/Cents)	:	EUR: 1,2 Cents: 1,2,5,10,20,50
9.	Exchange Rate (USD per EUR, as of Dec. 2012)	:	1.32
10.	Countries Using Euro as Currency	:	Andorra, Monaco, Montenegro, San Marino, and Vatican

Glossary

Appreciation

A currency is said to appreciate when it strengthens in price against another currency.

Adjustable peg

Some countries have pegged or fixed their currencies to a leading currency, such as the US dollar. However, they readjust the peg from time to time to make the currency more competitive. This arrangement is known as an adjustable peg.

Arbitrage

The simultaneous purchase and sale of a currency in order to take advantage of the price spread in a currency pair between the quotes of different brokers. The price spread is the difference between the bid and offer prices.

Ask price (Offer price)

The price at which a forex dealer is prepared to sell a currency. The ask price is also known as the offer price. For example, in the quote EUR/USD 1.3150/60, the base currency is EUR and the ask price is 1.3160. This means a customer can buy one EUR by paying 1.3160 US dollars.

Assignment

The notice to an option writer advising that the option sold was exercised by the buyer of the option.

At best

An instruction given to a forex dealer to buy or sell a currency at the best exchange rate that can be obtained.

At or better

An order to a forex dealer to buy or sell a currency at a specific price or better.

Authorised forex dealer

A dealer is a financial institution that has been authorised by a country's regulatory body to act as such by trading in currencies.

Aussie

Refers to the AUD/USD pair. This is also called *oz* or *ozzie.*

Base currency

Refers to the first currency in a currency pair. For example, in the quote EUR/USD, EUR is the base currency. This shows how much one EUR is worth as measured against USD.

Base rate

This is the minimum rate that a bank is allowed to charge its customers.

Basis point (bp)

This is the minimum change in the price quote for a currency. It is also called *pip.*

Bear market

Refers to a situation in which the price of a currency is consistently falling.

Bid price

The price at which a forex trader is willing to buy a currency. For example, in the quote EUR/USD 1.3150/60, the trader is willing to buy one euro against 1.3150 US dollars.

Bid-ask spread

The difference between the bid and ask price in a currency pair.

Bitcoin

A digital currency introduced in 2009. It is not regulated by any central bank. However several legal issues have come up recently regarding its existence. Bitcoin is traded on the Internet and based on peer-to-peer networks. Mt. Gox is the most established Bitcoin exchange. One Bitcoin is divided into 100 million smaller units, called satoshis, which are defined by eight decimal units.

Bretton Woods Agreement

An agreement established in July of 1944 at the United Nations Monetary and Financial conference held in Bretton Woods, New Hampshire, United States. The agreement established the adjustable, pegged foreign exchange rate system.

Bull market

A situation in which the price of a currency is consistently rising.

Bulls

Traders who hold long positions in a currency in anticipation of its growing strength.

Bureau de change

Bureau de change is an establishment where customers can convert one currency for another. In the United States, the term is not used; instead, the term is *money exchange* or *currency exchange.*

Cable

A slang term to denote the GBP/USD currency pair.

Call option

An option that gives the right to buy a currency at an agreed-upon rate on or before a specific date.

Carry trade

Currency carry trade refers to the act of borrowing one currency with a low interest rate in order to purchase another currency with a high interest rate to make an exchange profit.

Commodity currencies

Currencies of countries that are based on natural resources. They are the Canadian dollar, the New Zealand dollar, the Australian dollar, and the Russian ruble.

Concerted intervention

Coordinated action by a number of central banks in the forex market to control exchange rates.

Cross rate

A pair of currencies that does not include the US dollar.

Currency

Any form of money issued by a government or its central bank that is used as legal tender.

Currency pair

Two currencies that make up a foreign exchange rate. For example, USD/JPY.

Currency risk

Risk emanating from an adverse movement in exchange rates.

Currency code

The three-letter code representing a currency. The official currency codes are those issued by the International Standards Organisation.

Day trade

An opening and closing trade in a currency during a day.

Dealer

An individual or firm that acts as a principal or counterparty to a forex transaction.

Dealing spread

The difference between the bid and ask price of a currency.

Delivery date (settlement date)

The date on which both buyer and seller (of a currency trade) make physical delivery of the currencies. It is also known as the settlement date. Typically, the delivery date is two days after the trade date.

Depreciation

The fall in the value of a currency over time.

Derivative

A financial contract whose value is based upon the value of the underlying currency. Currency options and currency futures are examples of currency derivatives.

Devaluation

An official action to weaken a pegged currency.

Dovish

A data or monetary policy statement that suggests an easier monetary policy or lower interest rates.

DXY index (US dollar index)

An index to measure the value of the US dollar against the value of six foreign currencies (euro, Japanese yen, pound sterling, Canadian dollar, Swedish krona, and Swiss franc). The index was originally introduced by J.P. Morgan in 1973.

End of day order (EOD)

An order to buy or sell a currency at a specified price that is valid up to the end of the day (i.e., the end of market time).

Expiry date

The date on which a currency derivative (such as an option or a future) expires.

Fill or kill

A type of order to buy or sell a currency that gets cancelled if the order cannot be filled in its entirety.

Foreign exchange (forex or FX)

The simultaneous purchase of one currency and sale of another. It is also known as *forex* and *FX.*

Foreign exchange fixing

The daily monetary exchange rate fixed by the central bank of a country.

Forex signals

Forex trade alerts offered by experienced traders or forex analysts.

Forward points

The pips added to or subtracted from a spot exchange rate to produce the forward rate.

Forward rate

The rate for a foreign exchange contract settling at an agreed-upon future date. The rate is agreed upon when the contract is entered into.

Fundamental analysis

The study of macro and other underlying factors that influence a currency's exchange rate.

Futures contract

A contract to exchange a specified quantity of a currency at a set exchange rate at a future date. A future contract is traded in an exchange. The quantity, expiry date, and other terms of the contract are standardised as per the rules of the exchange.

Going long

The purchase of a currency for investment or speculation. The expectation is that the price will increase.

Going short

The sale of a currency that is not owned by the seller. The expectation is that the price will decrease.

Good for the day

An order to buy or sell a currency that will expire at the end of trading hours on that day if it is not filled.

Good till cancelled (GTC)

An order to buy or sell a currency that remains open until filled or cancelled by the customer.

Greenback

A nickname for the US dollar.

Hawkish

A data or monetary policy statement that suggests a tighter monetary policy or higher interest rates.

Hedge

A position in a currency that is intended to eliminate or reduce the risk of an existing position in a currency.

Interbank rates

The foreign exchange rates quoted between banks.

Inter-day trade

Trade that remains open overnight (or trade that is held over from one day to the next).

Intervention

Action by a central bank in the forex market to influence the exchange rate of its currency.

Intra-day trade

Trade that is opened and closed during the same business day.

Kiwi

A nickname for the New Zealand dollar.

Limit order

An order to buy a currency at a lower level than current market or to sell a currency at a higher level than the current market.

Long position

A position taken in a currency with the expectation that the currency will rise in value.

Loonie

A nickname for the Canadian dollar.

Market maker

A dealer who regularly quotes both bid and offer prices for a currency.

Market order

An order to buy or sell a currency at the current rate.

Market risk

The risk arising from changes in the market price of a currency.

Mark-to-market

The process of re-evaluating existing positions in a currency to determine margin requirements.

Offer (ask)

The price at which a currency dealer can sell a currency against the base currency in a currency pair. It is also known as the ask price. For example, in the quote EUR/USD 1.3150/60, the base currency is EUR and the offer price is 1.3160. This means that a customer can buy one euro by paying 1.3160 US dollars.

Option

A derivative that gives the right, but not the obligation, to buy or sell a currency at a set price before a specified date.

Over the counter (OTC)

A transaction that is not concluded through an exchange. In an OTC transaction, the trade takes place between two parties over the phone. Spot and forward forex trades take place in the OTC market.

Partial fill

A forex trade that is executed partially.

Percentage in point (pip)

The minimum fluctuation of an exchange rate. Most of the currency pairs (except Japanese yen) are quoted to four decimal places. For those currencies, a pip means one unit of the fourth decimal point. In the case of the yen, a pip means one unit of the second decimal point. In the case of the US dollar, euro, British pound, or Swiss franc, one pip is about 0.0001. In the case of the Japanese yen, one pip would be about 0.01.

Pound

A nickname for the British pound.

Premium

The amount by which the forward or futures rate exceeds the spot rate.

Put option

An option that gives the owner the right, but not the obligation, to sell a currency at a specified price before a specified date.

Revaluation

An official action by a government or central bank to strengthen a pegged currency.

Short position

A position in a currency pair in which the base currency is sold to benefit from a decline in its exchange rate.

Spot exchange rate

Spot exchange rate (aka spot rate) is the rate of a foreign exchange contract for immediate delivery. In other words, it is the current exchange rate at which a currency can be bought or sold. In the FX spot market, the delivery of a currency takes place within two days from the trade date. Spot trades are done on a T+2 settlement basis; i.e., settlement two days after the trade date. However, the settlement date will be extended to the next market day if there are any holidays in the countries of the currency pair or if there is a weekend between the trade and settlement days.

Spread

The difference between the bid and offer prices of a currency.

Sterling

A nickname for the British pound.

Stop order

An order to buy or sell a currency once a specified rate is reached. When the rate is reached, the order is executed at the best available price.

Stop loss order

An order to reduce the risk in a long or short position in a currency due to adverse movement in that currency. In the case of a long position, the stop loss order is to sell below the current price. In the case of a short position, the stop loss order is to buy above the current price. By setting a stop loss order, the potential loss in a currency position will be limited.

Street rate

Black market exchange rate.

Swap

A swap, in the context of foreign exchange (currency swap), is an agreement between two parties to exchange a principal amount and interest thereon in one currency in exchange for an equivalent principal and interest in another currency at a specified date and agreed-upon rate.

Swissy

A nickname for the Swiss franc.

Technical analysis

The study of the charts of past price movements of a currency to forecast the future direction of its price movements. Foreign exchange traders and speculators use technical analysis quite frequently to execute trades in various currencies.

Tick

The minimum change, either up or down, in a currency's exchange rate.

Tomorrow next (tom next)

In the foreign exchange market, *tomorrow next* is a procedure that involves the buying and selling of a currency to avoid taking actual delivery of that currency. This procedure is also called tom next.

Uptick

The price quote for a currency at a price higher than its preceding quote.

Value date

The settlement date of a currency transaction. In a spot forex trade, the value date is two business days after the trade date.

Volatility

A measure of a currency's fluctuation during a given period. It is expressed in percentage terms.

About the Author

Tholoor M Thomas is an experienced investment professional with over forty years of global investment management experience in all major asset classes, including foreign exchange. Thomas commenced his career in the foreign exchange department of India's premier bank, State Bank of India, in 1971. It was during the same year that the modern floating exchange rate regime came into effect. Thomas had hands-on experience with all facets of foreign exchange during his career with the bank. Later, he moved to the Middle East and served two large institutions. Thomas was employed for over thirty years in the investments and asset management department of a leading financial institution, Arab Insurance Group (Arig), in Bahrain. . As director of investments and asset management, Thomas played a decisive role in all aspects of multi-currency investments for a large, global portfolio. This activity included the management of sizable foreign exchange exposure.

He is a chartered financial analyst (CFA). He is a member of the CFA Institute in the United states and the CFA Society Bahrain. Thomas was the Annual Financial Forecast winner (CFA Society Bahrain) in 2010 and the winner of currencies forecast in the Citibank Treasury competition held in 1987.

Thomas is currently the managing director of ValueTree Consultancy W.L.L., a business consultancy firm in Bahrain.

About the Book

The foreign exchange (FX) market is the largest financial market and has a daily turnover close to five trillion US dollars. The evolution of the foreign exchange market since the abrogation of the Bretton Woods agreement in 1971 has been remarkable. The FX market, which was once accessible only to large banks and institutions, is now within reach of average people. This significant change stems from market liberalisation, globalisation, and advancements in technology. Most people carry out some sort of foreign exchange transaction very frequently—this transaction occurs directly or indirectly. Plus, the fluctuations in exchange rates affect the financial lives of people on a regular basis.

Yet the subject of foreign exchange is widely misunderstood because of its intricacies. It is essential to establish a basic understanding of FX because it has an important influence on our earnings, expenditures, savings, and investments. Though a lot has been written on the subject, much of the literature lacks precision. This book fills that gap by providing readers with a condensed and precise explanation of foreign exchange and its market dynamics.

Tholoor M Thomas draws on his forty-one years of experience in the foreign exchange market to introduce the forex basics, factors affecting exchange rates, exchange rate arithmetic, exchange rate regimes, options and futures used to hedge currency risks, evolution of the market through history, major market participants, numerous world currencies, and the key jargons used in the industry.

This book provides a wealth of information for students of finance, those looking to begin a career in foreign exchange, investment analysts, portfolio managers, and anyone interested in attaining a deeper knowledge of the foreign exchange universe.